# Living
## in
### the
# USA

| edited by

MARILYN MARQUIS **and** SARAH NIELSEN

One World
Many Voices
| a collection of student essays

One World Many Voices: Living in the USA
Copyright © 2010 by Marilyn Marquis and Sarah Nielsen

Published in the United States and the United Kingdom
by WingSpan Press, Livermore, CA

The WingSpan name, logo and colophon are the trademarks of
WingSpan Publishing.

ISBN 978-1-59594-414-6

First edition 2010

Printed in the United States of America

www.wingspanpress.com

Library of Congress Control Number 2010930633


1 2 3 4 5 6 7 8 9 10

This collection of essays, *Living in the USA*, about the joys and struggles of living in a new culture, is the fourth book in *One World Many Voices*, a series of collected essays written by and for English language learners. The series stems from an effort to provide easy and interesting extensive reading material for students in the ESL program at Las Positas College, in Livermore, California.

The editors of this series initiated READERS WRITING FOR READERS in 2006 to encourage students to write for readers who are learning English. By participating in READERS WRITING FOR READERS and reading the resulting books, students have the powerful experience of learning from peers and of helping others with their language development. Knowledge comes from students themselves. In reading the writing of their peers, students may simultaneously join a community of readers, discover themselves in the experiences of others, and expand their understanding of the world.

These student-generated essays, edited to control the variety of sentence structure and the range of vocabulary, provide high-intermediate level students with interesting, easy to understand material that they can read successfully without the use of a dictionary.

We wish to extend our thanks to the ESL faculty at Las Positas College for engaging their students in READERS WRITING FOR READERS. We are deeply grateful to the students for their genuine and creative contributions.

*Marilyn Marquis and Sarah Nielsen, editors*

# Acknowledgements

$\mathcal{W}$E ARE INDEBTED TO THE students in the English as a Second Language program at Las Positas College for their enthusiastic participation in READERS WRITING FOR READERS. Their heartfelt writing about their lives, their feelings, their families, their customs, and their struggles with living in a new country has inspired us to create this series of student-generated essays for their extensive reading.

We also want to acknowledge many others who have contributed to this series. Fredda Cassidy and the faculty and students in the Visual Communications program at Las Positas College worked patiently with us to establish the look and feel of these books. They designed the layout, logo, and covers through a truly collaborative process, in particular Linda Roberts, Rebecca Schoefer, Melinda Bandler, and Meg Epperly. Thank you!

Thank you also to the instructors in the English as a Second Language program at Las Positas College for inviting us into their classrooms to present READERS WRITING FOR READERS to their students and for encouraging their students to participate in the project.

We would like to acknowledge the contributions of individuals who offered feedback, suggestions, proofreading, and support, with special thanks to Dr. Philip Manwell, Dean of Arts and Communications at Las Positas College.

# Table of
# Contents

CHAPTER ONE

# Arrivals

Arriving Home

An Exciting Moment

Nightmare in My USA Life

The Long Journey to California

Stepping into the American Dream

 **Arrivals**

## Arriving Home

SARAH NIELSEN

*A*FTER I GRADUATED FROM COLLEGE in 1988, I was lucky to have the opportunity to live in Beijing, China, and work as an English teacher there for two years. By the late 80s, China had already been open to westerners for a number of years. However, even in a big city like Beijing, seeing a young, blonde American woman shopping in a farmer's market or riding her bicycle through the city's vast parks was something of a novelty back then.

Wherever I went in Beijing, people noticed me. Sometimes they stared as their mouths hung open in amazement or nudged their friends and pointed excitedly at me. Sometimes they asked to touch my hair or wanted to practice their English. Sometimes they would invite me—a total stranger—into their modest homes for elaborate meals. Occasionally, a man would shout "foreign devil" at me or rub up against me in a crowded bus in a way that made me feel very uncomfortable. Whether it was positive attention (most of the time) or negative attention (not very often), I felt like I was in the spotlight when I lived in Beijing. In fact, having all that constant attention was like being a famous movie star.

In the summer of 1990, I returned home to California to start the next chapter in my life. It was a bittersweet flight across the Pacific Ocean. I was sad to leave my second home, the cultural and political capital of China, a place where I had made many wonderful friends, learned to speak another language, and experienced living in a culture different from my own. At the same time, I was happy to return to family, friends and the familiar.

As the plane approached San Francisco, I could see the Golden Gate Bridge and the blue-green waters of the bay below me. My heart beat faster. My palms felt a bit sweaty. I was arriving home after being away for so long. What a warm and glorious welcome it would be! I imagined the cheering crowds, the smiling faces, the barrage of questions, and the bright flashing of cameras.

When I stepped off the plane, I noticed it right away. As I walked to baggage claim, waited for my luggage, and then went through customs, no one was looking at me. After I emerged from customs, I saw my family waiting for me. They hugged me and smiled and asked a lot of questions, but no one else was paying attention to me. As we made our way to the parking garage, same thing—nothing happened. No one wanted to take a picture with me or asked me where I came from. For a moment, I felt disoriented and disappointed, and then I had to laugh at myself. What was I really expecting? I was not a novelty or a foreign devil or a movie star. I was just plain old me. I had just arrived home, a place that would forever be familiar and foreign to me from that day forward.

# An Exciting Moment

OLIVERA PANIC

*My* FIRST EXCITING MOMENT RELATED to coming to the USA happened when I got my American visa. In my country, I had joined an au pair agency, which helps families to find nannies for their children and provides young women with the opportunity to experience living in America as well. The young women also have a chance to enroll in college while working as nannies. The family that I chose was from Pleasanton, California. They were a young couple with two beautiful children. I really liked the family already, and I couldn't wait for the day to finally meet them in person; however, at that moment, I was a little scared. Prior to arriving in the United States, I had talked to them a lot on the phone, and we knew a lot about each other, but I was still a little afraid. Fortunately, my fears were unfounded.

On April 16, 2007, I arrived at the San Jose International Airport. The family was waiting for me with the kids even though it was almost midnight. My heart throbbed very fast because I was excited like never before. When I got off the plane, first I saw my host mom holding a sign with my last name on it. Then I saw a little girl holding balloons. Both mother and daughter were looking at me with big smiles on their faces. I walked over to them, and we immediately hugged each other. At that moment, I knew I had made a good choice. I was excited to see the house and city where I would be spending my years, and luckily I liked everything that I saw.

The next morning we went to Bend, Oregon to celebrate my host mom's birthday. My host dad drove through half of California and Oregon, so I saw two states on my first full day in the United States, which was an amazing experience.

The family stopped in a couple of interesting places to show me the landscape of the west coast and introduce me to traditional American culture. I saw Indian sculptures made of wood, a big national park full of giant trees, and a beautiful lake on the border of California and Oregon. On the way to Bend, we also stopped by my host dad's family home, so I met that side of the family, too. They made a special Mexican meal for me, and that was the first time that I had tried Mexican food. After a few more hours of driving, we came to my host mom's family home. I was very excited by the beautiful house and its place up on the huge mountain where we were. I enjoyed every second of our trip.

All the people that I met on that trip were very nice, polite, and full of understanding for my not-so-good English. Everyone was interested in knowing more about Serbia and my family as well. From the time I got here until now, I have always had a good time with my host family. My experiences over two years have been more than great, so that is the reason I have decided to stay and study here. I like California and my friends, and I have enjoyed every moment spent in the United States.

## Nightmare in My USA Life

FRANCES WANG

THE MOST DIFFICULT THING I have been through in the USA is everything! I say this not only because English is my second language, but also because I have had to deal with overt racism, difficult personalities, and environmental differences. In public I have always felt the glare from people who recognize me as someone different. Maybe it is my delusion, but I came to this conclusion through a rather horrible experience when I first arrived in the United States a few years ago.

In spring 2005, I moved from Taiwan to the USA by myself in order to pursue my studies. My parents were worried about me, but they had busy schedules which they really needed to attend to. So they arranged for guardians in the United States who would pick me up from the airport and take me to their house. I wasn't that worried, and I told myself that it would be an incredible journey. Finally, when I arrived at the San Francisco International Airport, I felt a sense of relief from the pressure I'd been feeling. I thought I was almost at the end of a great adventure. After all, I imagined that I would take a nap in the host family's house and then start to unpack my baggage and organize my things. This turned out not to be the case.

When it was my turn to go through customs in San Francisco, I followed the white line for citizens and passed my United States passport to the officer at customs. This person, who I guessed was an ethnic minority but a native speaker of English, stared at me and looked back at my passport once again. I could tell he didn't trust me, a Chinese person with a United States passport. I was born in the United States, but I went back to Taiwan, where my family comes from originally. I had been living in Taiwan from the age of five, and I had lost most of my English skills. The customs officer asked me what my last name was, but I answered the question incorrectly, giving my first name instead. This was a huge but understandable mistake. In Taiwan, the family name comes first and is followed by the given name. In other words, in a Chinese name, the first name is the family name, and the last name is the given name, the exact opposite of English names where the last name is the family name and the first name is the given name.

The customs officer heard my answer and recognized the error, so he kept asking me questions. For instance, he asked me where I was born. "New York," I answered. But he didn't accept that answer and kept asking me, "New York WHERE?" I repeated the same answer several times, and I could feel tears welling up in my eyes. "But I was born here! I went back to Taiwan when I was so young that I forgot all my English. Why do I have to suffer like this?" I screamed this in my mind, of course, in Chinese. Because of my poor English and my darn Chinese personality, I couldn't even look him in the eye directly. I couldn't defend myself against him. I was frightened of him, like a sheep that could not resist a wolf's attack. I felt humiliated, either by him or by my own doing. "I should have studied more English before I came to this country where English is the main language," I thought regretfully.

My arrival here was difficult but helpful in that it inspired me to improve my English, even though it was a painful experience for me. I remain, however, fearful of American males, whom I always try to avoid.

## The Long Journey to California
### MARRAY PRINCESS CABUSAO

MOVING TO A NEW COUNTRY can be exciting, but it is also a time of major adjustments. It is a time for new experiences with different cultures and traditions. Since America is a multi-racial country, immigrants are drawn to it from every corner of the world, including the Philippines where I am from.

I remember growing up with bountiful blessings in life. Because my sister and I grew up with my maternal grandparents, we experienced the utmost love and care. Our uncle and aunt, my mom's brother and sister-in-law, were our secondary guardians, and spoiled us by fulfilling every wish. There was also a maid beside me whenever I needed help. My parents worked for a cruise ship company and were away a lot, but I always felt my mother and her family's kindness and support for me and my younger sister.

I was four years old when my parents separated and ended up divorcing. Since then, I haven't felt my father's caresses. My sister and I grew up without his presence or support. My mother has worked abroad continuously. When she began working for a company based in Miami, Florida, she would visit my uncle and his family in Livermore, California whenever she finished a contract.

My mom met my step-father in June 2002 in Livermore. I remember clearly my step-father's first visit to the Philippines. That was May 2003, the year I was in seventh grade and my sister in second. Our migration began in February 2006, when my mother got married to our good and loving step-father, a Filipino-American citizen in the United States Army.

Our secondary guardians in the Philippines, my uncle and aunt, took great care to help us prepare all our necessary documents. They even got up with us at 3 AM so that we could be first in the line of the thousands of passport applicants who waited every day to file their applications. I will never forget that. My own passport application was denied five times because I saw different evaluators every time, each of whom seemed to require yet another document. I experienced long queues while I gathered my other required documents from the National Bureau of Investigation, Police Clearance, National Census, and Saint Luke's Hospital. Thank God I finally got my passport issued after seven months.

The moment of truth finally came for my younger sister and me. Our visas were approved on September 5, 2008. We were both overwhelmed that day with feelings of joy and happiness. Because of the many hardships and trials we encountered over the two-year period that culminated in receiving our visas, we had built a greater confidence in ourselves and could fully savor the rewards of our efforts. We knew our journey to the USA would come soon.

At the American Embassy in Manila, the officials advised us to proceed to the Delivery Section to pay for our visas. We decided to pay extra for a rush delivery in order to receive our visas within five days, but we were unlucky and ended up waiting ten working days for our visas to arrive.

Once we had our passports and visas and had purchased our plane tickets, our parents sent a letter of consent to grant us permission to travel and be escorted by our neighbors to California. Since my sister was only twelve at the time and I only sixteen, we had to have our parents' approval to travel abroad as minors. My sister was the first one to depart. I followed her two weeks later because I had to finish my first semester as a nursing student in Manila.

I was very excited again on the day of my departure. I said farewell to all my family and friends, feeling a little sad because I knew I would be missing all of them. I got very nervous at the airport when my escort found out she had to pay a travel tax for her children. She didn't have enough money with her because she gave away all her cash to relatives in the Philippines. After several tense hours, she was able to reach her sister who lent her money for the travel tax. I felt relieved, and we boarded the plane just twenty minutes before take off.

On October 13, 2008, when I first arrived in California, I was welcomed by my family, whose hands were overflowing with flowers and balloons. I had my first dinner out in a great Japanese restaurant on that day of my arrival in California. In the days to come, I also got to dine out for lunch and dinner, experiencing Chinese, Korean, and other types of cuisine. I noticed right away that people here love to go out to eat and go shopping. I eventually learned about Black Friday and other holidays when there are many bargains to be had.

After my arrival, while I was dealing with the time change and jet lag, everyone else in my family would sleep at night. I was sleepless in the dark. After one week, I had adjusted to the new time. Unfortunately, it was not so easy for me to adjust to the chilly fall climate in Livermore. I had an allergic reaction all over my body because of the temperature difference. It took two months before my skin healed from the allergies. Another adjustment that was tough in those days just after my arrival involved doing chores whenever my mom asked me to. I was used to having a maid who did all those tasks, so I had a hard time responding quickly to my mom's requests at first. I am very lucky that my relatives were all supportive during those early days in California.

My migration here to California has been a great blessing. My family has taught me about the culture here and how to survive. I have developed a greater appreciation for how difficult life is in my native land and how hard people have to work to raise their children here as well. If you are new to the USA or California, remember that it will take time to understand the new culture and realize that it is neither all good nor all bad. I received some advice when I first arrived. It helped me a lot in the months after my arrival. I am learning from that advice, and I hope you will, too.

I am learning to try hard to overcome obstacles, to laugh at my mistakes, and to praise myself when I learn from them. I am learning to appreciate nature, to enjoy the flowers, and to keep the calmness of a sunny day. I am learning to greet strangers and to enjoy my friends. I am learning to embrace my emotions and to be unafraid to show them. All these things help me live my dreams.

## Stepping into the American Dream
### DETELINA IVANOVA

THE LAND OF FREEDOM, THE land of dreams, the land of unlimited opportunities—that's what I had heard about the United States before my arrival here. I was skeptical then and believed that it was just a myth, that people were exaggerating. But a few years after I immigrated to America, I was telling my friends back in Bulgaria, "I'm living my dreams! I found the best opportunities I could have ever imagined!"

For the first time in our lives, my husband and I stepped on American land in March 2000. After one night's flight time, we appeared in the Silicon Valley, the world center of advanced technologies. Our friends, who already lived here in San Jose, California, helped us in our first month with accommodations and useful advice about how to begin our new life here. We both had a good education and technical skills, so it wasn't long or hard to find our first jobs in a laser company two weeks after our arrival. At the end of our first month here, we moved to our first rental apartment in a beautiful neighborhood in Mountain View. We enjoyed the sunny and pleasant California weather. On the weekends, we were swimming in the pool and relaxing in the jacuzzi. The difference in the living standards was shocking. Back then, Bulgaria was undergoing difficult economic times, and for scientists like us, it was very hard to meet even basic living costs. Both of us had worked two jobs at a time, earning just enough money to cover the bills and have some food in the fridge.

Arriving here felt like a magical relief from the hardships we had faced in Bulgaria. We felt like we were living our dreams. We were traveling every weekend, eager to get to know better the country which welcomed us so warmly and which was about to become our new homeland. The first place we visited was the Golden Gate Bridge in San Francisco. People visiting here for the first time always ask me why it is called golden if it is not made from gold. That was my first question when I saw it for the first time. And I think that the answer is that people have their own interpretation depending on where they are coming from as they approach the bridge. To me, it symbolizes a golden gate that opens to the path of fulfilled dreams and to the horizon of new ones.

A few months after my arrival, I found a job in my professional field as a research associate in the Navy Postgraduate School in Monterey, California. I felt immense gratification returning back to scientific research. My husband was hired as a software engineer in a biotechnology company in Sunnyvale. Our lives improved with every passing day. There was no doubt for us that we found in America the best opportunities of our lives. For two years now, I have been working as a postdoctoral researcher in one of the most famous United States national laboratories. I never ever even imagined in my life that I would get to work with such high technology in such an advanced scientific environment.

Looking back on our arrival and that exciting first year of new beginnings from the perspective of the current economy in a worldwide recession, not all of my pathways as a first-generation immigrant seem to be dreamlike and pleasant. Nowadays I am wondering if I will be able to find a job next year when my contract with the present employer finishes and if I will be able then to pay the mortgage for the house I am living in. But as the ancient Chinese wisdom says, every crisis is a new beginning, and I am optimistic and prepared for the next big change in my own and my family's life. With the current market and energy crises, in a changing global climate, we are facing the biggest challenges in our lives. I believe that the United States is destined to lead the rest of the world in a green revolution through the creation of new technologies. These technologies will create a new infrastructure supplied by alternative energy resources based on solar, wind, and water power. I am excited to be part of the scientific community, which is determined to work hard to find the ways and the means to create a new lifestyle, transforming us into a society where we will produce and consume while caring for the environment of our home Earth.

CHAPTER TWO

# Opportunities

 **Opportunities**

## Understanding the American Dream

SARAH NIELSEN

*I*WAS BORN TO AMERICAN PARENTS outside the United States. Our family moved back to California when I was just over a year old. Like so many others inside and outside the United States, I grew up believing that this country was a land of opportunities, a place where anyone with a dream, determination, and a little luck could be successful and live a great life. As I matured, learned more about American history, and gained more experience in the world, I discovered that the American Dream was often more of a myth than a reality. I began to ask myself how the American Dream could exist if this country enslaved people, took their property away, or restricted their access to education.

It was with these types of questions in mind that, as a new ESL teacher, I asked my advanced students to write something called a critical autobiography. To complete the assignment, students had to draw on research as well as their own life experiences to come up with a theory explaining how the American Dream worked. To prepare for the assignment, our class did a lot of reading about the American Dream, most of which was critical of this notion. In fact, much of the reading suggested the American Dream was a myth used by the rich and powerful to control other people.

In my class of twenty-five students, one student did theorize that the American Dream was an important mechanism for getting people to work hard with the hope of hitting it big. If people didn't make it, they would believe they did not work hard enough. They did not consider other factors that might limit their success, factors such as racism, classism, sexism, or homophobia.

The twenty-four other students in the class saw the American Dream in a much more positive light. As a group, they had endured and overcome the worst aspects of human societies: war, disease, famine, oppression, and poverty. For them, the possibilities that the American Dream opened up gave them hope and courage to confront the struggles they faced in their own lives. For these students, the possibilities promised by the American Dream were powerful because they meant that change could and did happen for individuals, communities, and societies.

There are still many problems and inequities in American society that need to be addressed, but my students helped me see that this is, indeed, a nation of opportunity, a place that gives hope to the hopeless, a space where new possibilities can open up at anytime.

## American Life: Myth and Reality

NGOCHIEN THI VO

*M*OST PEOPLE LIVING IN ASIAN countries think that American life is the best life in the world. They believe that when they go to the United States, they can easily enjoy the comforts of life in this country. However, once people arrive here, many fall into desperate situations and have to work hard just to make ends meet. They discover that it isn't easy to enjoy the comforts of life in the United States. For me, I knew from the beginning that I would have to start a new life in the United States from scratch. I knew it wouldn't be easy, even though my husband sponsored me to come here. Today I am proud of myself because I have overcome the initial difficulties, and I have gradually integrated into American life.

I have been living in the United States since October 1999. Although I had studied English in my country and read many books about America, everything here was totally different than what was in my mind. I faced new and strange experiences during the first couple of months. For example, America is a big country with many freedoms, diverse cultures, and many languages spoken by the people. There are people here from every country of the world, and it's a pleasure to meet so many people of different races in one country. There are also many places to visit. San Francisco has Chinatown and Japantown. Los Angeles has Little Saigon. In some parts of the United States, there are high mountains or vast lowlands. Other parts are deserts.

My husband has helped me adjust to living in the United States. When I first arrived, he showed me how to pay for goods using a card, how to find the supermarket, how to communicate with people around me, and how to use the phone to call my friends or get assistance in an emergency. In Vietnam, I could communicate easily with people and knew how everything worked. I had to learn a new way here.

When I first immigrated to the United States, I had no job. One week after my arrival, my husband helped me to enroll in the International Cosmetology and Beauty College in Oakland in order to get a manicurist license. During the first weeks of my study, my husband drove me to school. Later I caught a ride with one of his friends and eventually learned how to take the bus to school. Even something like taking the bus wasn't easy at first. Despite some communication difficulties due to my accent in English, I talked to the bus driver to find out how to pay for the bus ticket and how to signal for him to stop. After four months, I passed the driving test and got a driver license, which gave me more independence and changed my life for the better.

I am proud of myself for gradually integrating into American life. After getting my driver license, my husband bought me a new car. Not long after that, I passed the manicurist examination and received my license. I got a good job in a beautiful salon in Dublin. To improve my English skills, I enrolled in ESL classes at the College of Alameda. Two years later, I gave birth to my first son, and a second son came soon after. At that time, I had to quit school and stay home to take care of my children.

I am also very happy because three years ago I brought my parents here from Vietnam. They have helped me take care of my children so that I could go back to school and improve my English skills. However, I know there is still a lot to learn about living in the USA. For example, I need to learn more about American culture, holidays, and the educational system here. Because my children were born here, I have to learn about these things and teach them to become good students and good citizens of America.

I feel proud that I have risen above difficulties and become part of the American life. Nothing is as difficult as it might seem at first if we try to do our best and work hard in shaping our new life.

## The End of the World, California
LILA GHORBANALISHAH

IT WAS A COLD NIGHT in January 1993 in Tehran, Iran. The telephone rang, and I picked up the phone. My sister-in-law, who had become a citizen of the United States, called me for information she needed to help us apply for a United States green card. I gave her all the necessary information which she needed to fill out our application. I hung up the phone, but could not imagine that one day I would leave my country and my relatives, and would live in a foreign country, a place called "The End of the World" or "The Land of Opportunities."

In December 2006, a new chapter of my life started when my family and I moved to the End of the World, California, America. I was shocked like a person with a concussion. During the first two weeks after our arrival, everything happened very fast. We registered our children in their schools, rented an apartment, bought some cooking supplies and bedding, and took our driving tests. I even got my first job in America as a cashier in a store.

In those early days, I used to get lost easily, so I always had the map of our city with me. I was confused by the new calendar since it was different than the Iranian one. For a while, everything was strange to me: streets, huge stores, smiling people who didn't know me but said hello anyway.

My family has also had to adjust to differences in our lifestyle. We were used to living in a large house in Iran because we have a large family. Now in America, we live in an apartment. This has caused some arguments between my children because they have to share a room. For example, my daughter has to study late into the night and needs the light on. On the other hand, my son wants to sleep and needs the light off. My husband and I sadly witness their disagreements and their complaints about each other.

Another problem we have faced is my husband's job. He has owned his own business for a long time, and he does not like to work for others as an employee. During the past two years, he has been looking for a new business to start in the United States, and we have had some difficulties with our expenses as well. Despite these difficulties, day by day I have learned new things, and I am getting to know my talents better and better. And now I have come to have two essential reasons for living in the United States.

My first and most important reason is my children. Living in a better place, where there are many opportunities, is the dream of most people around the world. How lucky I am that I can raise my children in this land where they can feel freedom, where they can find a path of their own choosing, not one forced on them by the family or the judgment of society, where being superior depends on their knowledge. They are being raised in a country where most people are open-minded and progressive. My children will have more choices for finding their abilities which are hidden inside of them, and which they might not know anything about otherwise. For example, math was a hard subject for my daughter in Iran. She had good grades, but she just memorized formulas. In contrast, in America, she understands math completely, and solving math problems is one of her favorite hobbies now.

Another reason that I continue living in the United States is for myself. It may be interesting for you to know that I am back at school after twenty-six years. Education has always been important to me, and for a silly reason, I could not continue my academic pursuits in Iran. I should remind readers that after the revolution in Iran, all schools were separated into those for boys and those for girls. When I was a senior in high school, I had a simple argument with the new principal about wearing a head scarf inside the classroom. I refused to wear a scarf while in the classroom, and my reason was logical. All the people in the class were females, but she insisted on her idea. I had this problem with the principal for two months. Then one day when she was checking the classrooms, she came to our class. All the other girls wore their scarves. I was the only one without. She saw me with my scarf around my neck. "Why don't you have your scarf on?" she demanded. "I am deaf and cannot hear when something covers my ears," I replied. She thought I was making fun of her. Honestly, I was tired of her attitude. She was extremely strict about silly rules, yet she had no awareness of her own bad behavior. Unfortunately, the simple argument had no result other than to lower my citizenship grade from an A+ to a D, a black spot on my otherwise good academic record of twelve years. Because of this, I could not pass the moral test for the university, which is given annually in Iran.

I am satisfied that I live in the United States now. Obviously, I have had many problems in my new life here including missing my parents, my motherland, and forty years of good memories. But all people, no matter where we are, face problems. What is important is how we face and adapt to our own difficulties, how we learn to solve the problems of our lives.

In my opinion, knowledge can change our point of view and even our lives. With knowledge, we can solve problems better. With knowledge, we can positively affect ourselves, our family, our society, and finally our world. With education, we can have a better world for all human beings. Here, in America, we have more opportunities for better lives and for promoting education in different fields. In short, I can say I am thankful to live in America even with all the problems I have because I know I can find better resolutions for my problems and can help my world more when I live among progressive people.

## Building a Better Future

MIRYAM MATAMET

MOVING TO THE USA WAS one of the most difficult decisions of my life. It was also one of the best. When I first came here, I didn't know how long I would stay. I didn't even know if I could learn the language quickly. I did know, however, that I liked it here. And I knew I would have some new opportunities as well.

Learning English has been a challenging process, although it has been rewarding. When I first came here, I couldn't understand what people were talking about. It was frustrating. A friend told me about the ESL program at Las Positas College. When I started taking classes, I began to learn more quickly. I also met some friends and had some good teachers. Now I can read the newspaper and understand much of what I read. This has really helped my self-confidence. I still have a lot to learn, but I am enjoying the process.

Living here has also given me a better lifestyle. I chose to live in the East Bay because I have friends here, including some native speakers. I like the area a lot because it is clean and organized, and there is a lot to do. I feel that it is a safe place to live as well, and I have a job here.

Perhaps most importantly, living in the USA has given me hope for a better future. I want to finish the ESL program and then enroll in either a teaching or nursing program. I really like to help children, so this is one of my goals. Hopefully, I can use my new language and my native language because I know that bilingual people are preferred in the job market, especially in California.

I feel like moving to the USA was a good decision for me. I have had to make some sacrifices and overcome some fears, but it has been worth it. I believe this country has the most opportunities for me and holds a place for my future. By learning English and working hard, I know I can make my dreams come true.

## The New Me
FREDDY ALVAREZ

COMING TO THE UNITED STATES was a bittersweet moment for me as I left my friends back in my country, Mexico. I recall that I didn't tell anyone I was moving to another country in order to join my parents who wanted me to be with them. My grandparents eventually told all my friends about my move when they started asking about me. Coming to the United States has changed me in many ways. I can see where my future is going, and my mind is wide open for what's coming next. This is a new me.

Coming to the United States has made me grow into the person I am now. It has made me strong. Today, I can identify all the evil around me and protect myself from it. When I moved here to the United States, my parents warned me not to fall into any temptations, not to take up any vices such as smoking or drinking because this is a country where most young people my age are prone to these sorts of behaviors. My parents were quite protective, as they experienced that with my older brother, Luis. Once I turned 18, my mother told me that it was up to me whether I chose the right or wrong way. Whatever path I choose to take, I'd better look twice. I want to see the right one, the one that won't affect me in any negative way. Due to my knowledge of what's good and bad, I can protect myself from harmful people. I can either fight or talk, but I will always keep surviving with more knowledge and power. Being young and seeing new things every day will help me use my experiences to be a better man.

My experiences in the United States have taught me many things, but the most important is the English language. In my country, English must be learned as a foreign language, which is quite difficult because students only practice at school. They only learn the basics; the teaching of pronunciation and writing is poor. Even though my school in Mexico had an American teacher to teach students the language, it wasn't the same as learning it in the United States. Here I have to use English every day in order to communicate with people. My language and learning skills have both improved rapidly because I'm here in America surrounded by English.

Living in the USA has not only helped me as an individual person, but it has also brought me closer to my parents. Back in my country, Mexico, we didn't have as much communication as we do now. Mexico is a closed-minded country where people with different opinions or feelings have to be quite careful not to show these differences to the larger community because of the discrimination they would experience. To me, coming to the United States was an emotional relief because I knew America to be a free country where people don't criticize or humiliate others. Everyone has rights here. My orientation to have feelings for the same sex didn't change my parents in any way. They have supported and accepted me without changing their feelings towards me. They understand that this is who I am and who I want to be. This is me. My parents have left their traditional beliefs behind and opened their minds to a new world where I could fit in and be happy. They too have gotten used to the American life of freedom. My family is quite close, and no one is ashamed of expressing feelings or opinions.

In brief, coming to the United States has changed me in many ways, for I can see where my future is going and my mind is wide open for what's coming next. This is a new me. Having no vices, learning English, and feeling happy are some ways that America has taught me to grow in the right way. I feel strong enough to protect myself from harmful people or evil without depending on someone else. In addition, I am improving my English skills by practicing every day in the United States, and I am closer to my family as they approve of my sexual orientation and don't feel ashamed of who I am.

THE UNITED STATES IS A well known land of opportunity. It is so generous, accepting all kinds of people who come from different parts of the world regardless of race or religious beliefs. It has opened its arms to everyone who has come here in the last few centuries and continues to do so as people come for many different reasons. Because of political and economic hardship in their homelands, refugees continue to arrived from many different parts of the world. Most of these people who arrived in their new country have had to face many obstacles, adjusting to a new language, learning new job skills, and taking care of families at the same time.

Living in a new country is a big challenge for new immigrants, who are not used to living in such a different environment. They need to start everything anew; the first thing is language. I remember when my husband and I arrived at the San Francisco airport on July 8 in the mid 1970s. It was so cold while we were waiting for a sponsor representative to pick us up. Of course, when Tom arrived, we could not say much of anything because of the language barrier, though he saw us shaking and he understood how we felt. We got to San Francisco after five o'clock in the afternoon, and it was a shock to us. The big city sat on a hill, and the agency that sponsored us had rented an apartment in the Nob Hill area for us. As the first Cambodian refugees to arrive here in the city of San Francisco, we were surprised beyond our imagination.

That night we could not sleep because of the time change, the city noise, and jet lag. We were also worried about our future, which we could not communicate to other people. Therefore, we asked each other, "How can we learn English?" I remember we said to each other, "We survived for 21 days without food during our escape, and we will again." The next morning, Tom, who picked us up at the airport, came again and told us that we were going to school. It was the answer to a good dream that we had wished for over a long time. When we heard the word "school," my husband and I were so happy. First, Tom showed us how to buy tickets and take the bus to school. After we arrived at Alemeny Adult School in San Francisco, which was about three miles from our apartment, Tom helped us to enroll in an ESL class. School went very well. We were young, and our memory was good and our determination strong. Everything seemed to be going well until one day my husband decided to walk home from school to save the twenty-five cent bus fare. Unfortunately, he was stopped by a man with a knife who asked for change. My husband did not have much money, so he gave the man some of the money he had. However, he wanted it all and attacked my husband. The lesson we learned was that living in a big city, not knowing the language, and trying to be good to others meant facing difficulties.

To make matters worse, we did not know how long the agency would continue to support us with fifty dollars a week; therefore, getting a job was always in our mind. Two and half months later, the agency found a job for my husband in a pizza restaurant. It was very difficult for both of us because he only made $2.50 per hour. He also came home late and had to wake up early in the morning to go to school. Living in downtown San Francisco was a big challenge. Everything was so expensive, so we found a roommate who was willing to share an apartment in the Sunset District. Life was even harder when we worked late at night and had no transportation. My husband had to walk from Geary Boulevard, which was on the other side of the Golden Gate Park, to Lincoln Avenue where we lived. One night he came home about 3 AM with his hand tied to his neck because he had injured his hand at work and had gone to the emergency room. I was only 21 years old then, horrified by not knowing what to do. Living in a new country where we did not speak the language and had no job skills was extremely difficult.

In addition to attending school and getting a job, I also wanted my family to be together again. My only surviving brother was still in Thailand. I regretted that I did not protect him from the Thai military, who took him away from us when we escaped to Thailand. I remember begging my sponsor for help to bring him to this country. It took two years to finally find him in the refugee camp, and we reunited soon after that. By that time, my husband and I had gone for job training. He had gotten a better job, and I was working, too. Because of my husband's job, we had moved to Union City. Everything went well for about a year until my brother George came. We were evicted from our apartment where minors were not allowed to live. In those days, there wasn't a law to protect families with children. Raising and supporting a family can be a big responsibility. We needed a good paying job to provide an education and a place to live, which was also very difficult.

Above all, living in a new country, learning a new language, getting a good job and supporting a family were life learning lessons for me. It made me a strong person, someone who can forgive and move on to the future.

# My New Life in the United States

MARIELA ALFARO

*My* life changed suddenly and unexpectedly a few years ago. When my family and I lived in Colombia, my husband worked as a police officer for twenty-two years. In October 1999, my oldest daughter was kidnapped by guerrillas. After ten days, she was rescued by a group of police. At that time, my husband was working in a special anti-drug unit with the United States government. After the kidnapping, the American government offered our family protection and the chance for a new life in the United States.

My daughter and I left Colombia first because we were still the targets of guerrilla warfare. At that time, we felt very confused and sad, for we had never imagined that our lives would change so dramatically. After six months, my husband and my other two children arrived in the United States.

It was a tough life because we had to begin everything again in this new country. We had to find a house, and we each had to find a job. In our family, my son was the only one who could speak English. The rest of us only spoke Spanish. We looked for jobs in different places, but the employers required good spoken English skills. Because of this, we were only able to find hard jobs such as housekeeping, dishwashing, construction, and janitorial work. For three years, my husband, my son, my older daughter and I worked in different jobs.

The American government helped support us for the first three months we lived here, which we appreciated, but we felt pressure to save money in case of an emergency. So, despite all the long hours and hard work, my husband and I were constantly very worried about our economic situation. We prayed a lot.

One day my son suggested that I start my own catering company. My son helped me find an organization called the New America Corporation, which helps immigrants to start their own small businesses. I studied for one year and graduated in small business and business planning. In addition to my formal studies, I had experience to draw on because my parents had owned a restaurant where I worked for several years. Once I started my catering business here, the whole family worked in the business because most of the catered events were scheduled for the weekend.

I had my catering company for five and a half years. I eventually sold the company because I had a lot of stress and got so sick that I could not continue working. While I was in treatment, my doctor suggested that I relax and eat well. She told me about some excellent vitamins and showed me research about the products which were made using new nanotechnology. The name of the company that makes these products is RBC Life Sciences. These vitamins helped stabilize my body, and I feel strong and healthy again. I did my own research on these products, and the company invited me to work with them.

During those early years in the United States, my life changed little by little, and it continues to change. Now my children are pursuing their own careers. My oldest daughter works as an economist at Saint Mary's College. My son is a business manager at Holy Names University and will graduate from Golden Gate University Law School in San Francisco in the spring. My youngest daughter is studying for a political science degree at Boston University and plans to graduate next year.

I am now continuing my education, too. I am studying English because the company wants me to speak English better. In fact, my husband and I agree that this is our time to concentrate on learning English. We give thanks to God for our lives, and we are thankful to live in the United States.

## Old Woman

LUCIA PAPALE

IN THE SUMMER OF 1996, I arrived in Miami, Florida, from Cali, Colombia. I was very excited to visit this country again after twelve years of not being here. I had lived in New York in 1984 for almost a year and had the opportunity to learn about American culture. When I came to this country that summer of 1996, I was already convinced that America was the country where I wanted to live my life as an "old woman." To make my decision, I analyzed and compared when and how women are considered "old" in Colombia and in the United States. I focused on two main considerations: establishing a loving relationship and finding opportunities to work.

One aspect I compared was the age for marriage. In Colombia, the cultural perception is that a woman who is not married in her twenties is already over the hill. The society puts a lot of pressure on women to marry. For example, if you are thirty years old and single, everyone is asking you the same question: Do you have a boyfriend? If you say yes, then they respond with a question and a comment: When are you getting married? You know, time goes by fast and you are getting old. If you say you don't have a boyfriend, they give dire warnings: You'd better hurry and find one; you're getting old. Given this societal pressure, you can imagine what would happen if you were unmarried in your forties or fifties. It is almost impossible for women of that age to establish a serious relationship and get married. In contrast, here in America, women are never too old to get married or find a serious, loving relationship. I have found that almost all American women have a positive mental attitude in this matter. When it comes to love, they never feel old. Cultural pressures to marry by a certain age don't seem to exist here. Therefore, women feel that it is never too late to find someone, even for people who were born in a different culture and live here in the United States now. This attitude is contagious. For instance, the mother of one of my Colombian friends got married in her eighties when she came to the United States after being single for almost fifty years in Colombia. I have also caught this "disease," and I am now a happily married "old woman."

Another aspect I considered in coming to America was the possibility of getting a job regardless of my age. In Colombia, even when women have skills to bring to the job market, it is difficult to find a good job when they are in their thirties. One example of this can be seen in local newspapers. Job announcements might say something like "Administrative assistant needed. 18-25 years old." It is legal in Colombia for an employer to ask for your age on your resume. If you get laid off from a job in your forties, it is almost impossible to get hired again. For instance, one of my friends in Cali, Colombia, was a sales manager for ten years. In 2001, the company she worked for laid her off. After all this time, she still hasn't found a new job. As soon as the employer reads her age, she is immediately disqualified for the position. This discrimination against age, especially for "old women" in Colombia, had a profound effect on my decision to come here. In contrast, in America it is illegal and considered discrimination to ask a person's age when she applies for a job. As a result, any woman has a chance to find a job and work anytime in her life regardless of her age. One of the things that impressed me the most when I went to Florida was to see all these "old women" working in different positions and contributing to the larger society. In observing this, I felt reassured that I had made the right decision. Today, after twelve years of living here, I am proud to have developed my own practice working as a massage therapist and esthetician.

Now I am happy to be an "old woman" loving and working in America, a place where you are never too old to do anything.

# Difficult Transitions

# Difficult Transitions

## Moving to a New Culture

MARILYN MARQUIS

IN THE SUMMER OF 1980, my family hosted two exchange students through an international exchange program, The Experiment in International Living. The first, a young woman from Japan who had recently graduated from high school, arrived in southern California with a large contingent of Japanese students for a four-week stay. The organization arranged dinners, concerts, and sporting events for the students and their host families. I enjoyed meeting these young people, who were full of curiosity and enthusiasm, and the other host families, who shared my interest in world cultures. Our guest student was eager to teach our family about Japan and to learn about the United States, California style. She was amazed by the grocery stores, the freeways, the houses, family life, and teenager behavior, especially the tradition of toilet-papering friends' houses. Every night after my daughters went to bed, Yoko and I would sit with her Japanese-English dictionary and discuss her experiences of the day. She always had a list of questions about family life, work life, and student life. In the process, she taught me as much about Japan as I taught her about English and living in the United States.

Our second student that summer was a young woman from France who was entering graduate school in the fall and wanted to have some time with an American family before living independently near the university campus. Martine had already experienced traveling throughout Europe and had traveled to the United States. Her preference was to communicate as much as possible in English prior to the start of classes. We enjoyed our month together, and I learned how to get a student ready for college. We bought a used car, found an insurance agent, found a house for her to share with some other graduate students, and settled into a lovely routine of visiting almost every weekend. Our friendship has continued for many years.

Hosting these two visitors inspired me to become an ESL teacher. I enjoyed talking about the language, my language, in a very different way. The questions that each one asked about the language fascinated me and afforded me the opportunity to recognize some of those very confusing aspects of English that frustrate English language learners. I discovered that I also enjoyed learning about other cultures and explaining mine. I found the perfect profession for myself.

I enrolled in a graduate program in 1981 to learn how to teach English as a second language and began teaching at a private school for Japanese businessmen in 1982. I loved my new profession. When I started teaching at Long Beach City College in 1983, I encountered large classes with immigrants from around the world, but most were from Mexico and

Vietnam. This is where I first encountered students writing and talking about the difficulties of moving to a new country. They wrote about the struggles of finding a job, going to the doctor's office, meeting new friends, and communicating in English. I listened attentively and thought I understood their experiences, but when I moved in 1991 to teach at Las Positas College, I realized how difficult it is to move away from a community of family and friends.

Before I left southern California, I was very excited about moving to the Bay Area and starting my new job at Las Positas College, the newest community college in California. I was the first ESL teacher at the college and would have the opportunity to create and build a new program. I never thought about how much I might miss my old life because my new life seemed so inviting. I thought that culture shock only happened when people moved to another country.

On the first night in my home, I was sad and lonely, and my daughter was no help because she also felt lonely. We both missed our friends and familiar community. We wondered why we had wanted to move so far from home. We both struggled to feel at home in our new home.

When I went to the bank or the grocery store or the library, no one said hello or seemed glad to see me. I was a stranger to everyone. After living in one community for many years, I knew the parents and brothers and sisters of my children's friends, so every where I went, I encountered friendly faces and could enjoy conversations about their lives. I also knew where to buy the perfect birthday gift for a friend or have my shoes repaired. Here I knew no one. No one honked and waved as I walked through town. I felt terribly lonely and friendless. I realized that my feelings of isolation and loneliness were very similar to those that my students had described to me. Most of them thought that the language barrier was the most significant problem, but I discovered that even though I could speak the same language as everyone around me, I still felt homesick.

When classes started in the fall and I was once again in an ESL classroom with my students, I finally felt at home again. It took several years for me to establish myself in my new community. Even though I enjoyed working with some wonderful people, no one at work really knew me or my family. We shared no history and had no common experiences. I discovered that the comfort of feeling at home comes from much more than having a place to live and work.

## The USA is Changing Me
ANONYMOUS

THE UNITED STATES IS VERY different from my country, Vietnam. When I left Vietnam for the USA about a year ago, I had to make only a few changes, but those changes had a major effect on my life. I had to learn to make new friends and to spend my time in very different ways.

In Vietnam, I used to have a lot of friends, and most of them were very dear friends. For example, my best friend in high school was a girl whom I could talk to for hours without ever feeling bored. We encouraged and advised each other in many ways. People often thought we were a couple, but we were not. We were the rarest of friends. The style of living in Vietnam allowed me and my friends to meet together everyday, which promoted close relationships.

When I was with my relatives in Vietnam, I always told them a lot of fun stories and made them laugh a lot. So everyone, especially people my same age, felt happy when talking to me. Unfortunately, my relatives, who have lived in the USA for a long time, don't speak Vietnamese very well. When I am with them, they speak English and speak very fast. So what can I do? I can simply sit and keep quiet. My American relatives are very kind people, and I hope to be able to communicate with them and make them happy when they talk to me.

Now I live in the United States and also have many new friends, but I still feel lonely even though most of my new friends are Vietnamese students, too. I think the reason is we haven't known each other for a long time and haven't spent a lot of time together. Sometimes we don't understand each other. I thought I would become friends with some American people, but I have felt uncomfortable with my English and afraid to talk to them.

Since coming to the United States, I have had to make some big changes in my daily life. I liked to hang out and drink coffee with my friends in the evening when I lived in Vietnam. I remember my friends and I drank coffee almost every day. For about half an hour each day, we amused each other with stories and ideas. We often drank coffee outside on the sidewalk, which is very popular in my country. But now I just drink coffee in the morning. I go to the coffee shop on the way to school. I drink my coffee. That's it. How boring is that? I no longer have time to enjoy coffee with friends. The taste of the coffee and the social aspect of drinking it have changed totally.

I have also had to give up playing video games since coming to the USA. In my country, I played video games a lot. But now I consider the importance of time, so I don't waste my time playing games anymore. Actually, I do not have very much time for leisure activities because now I have to work, go to school, and do my homework, which consume most of my time.

One new experience I have had in the United States is at work. When I first started working at my job, the manager was so kind to me. I remember the early school days; she drove me to school in the morning and picked me up in the afternoon until I could take the bus by myself. She treats me as well as she would her own son. I have never met anyone like her before.

I have had to give up some of my favorite activities, but I think it's good for my future. I don't know what turns my life will take, but when I came to America, a lot of things in my life changed. I think I will try to accept them.

## My Precious American Friends

OLGA KNKADE

$\mathscr{A}$s THE TIME TO FLY to America approached, my worrying increased. I wondered how I would adapt to the new country, how I would make new friends, and how I would live my life in English. I entertained many negative thoughts and fears during those days. I didn't know what to expect from my new life. I certainly didn't expect that the birds in my new garden would help me to avoid culture shock in the United States.

I arrived in the USA at night and was very tired after my long journey, so I went to sleep as soon as we arrived home. When I woke up, my husband and I went to drink tea in the garden. Everything was new and strange for me. All seemed beautiful, but tears rolled from my eyes. Deep sadness at leaving my native Ukraine was squeezing my sensitive heart. I wanted to be home.

As I sat longing for the familiar sounds and sights of home, a bird appeared from nowhere. Even now, I remember all of the details of her. She sat on the apple tree branch and stared at me. She was like a messenger from nature to settle me down. Never had I seen such an indescribably beautiful bird, and I fell into my child's fairyland. The bird had an unusually bright red color. She held her head proudly on a long neck, like a ballerina. Her vivid black eyes were bewitching me. My tears were mysteriously gone, and my heart filled with warmth and happiness. Every morning I went to the garden with my tea and waited for my dear friend. Soon, I was admiring other birds as I waited for her, asking, "Where are you?"

I recalled a time from my childhood when my father made bird feeders for the cold winters. He taught me that we need to support nature during difficult freezing winters when everything was blanketed in snow. This remembrance gave me the idea to have a feeder. I thought that if I hung it in my garden, birds would come to me often.

When I asked my husband, a big nature lover, to make a feeder, he did it with great pleasure. Then we bought seeds and waited for the birds. Several days passed, but no one came. I began to feel upset, but I never lost hope, and finally they came to me! First, there was one sparrow. Later, he probably brought his family, too. Over time, there were more and more birds. They had blue, grey, yellow, and brown colored feathers. I was curious about their names and found a guide to northern California birds. I concluded that our feeder hosted mockingbirds, scrub jays, pigeons, doves, warblers, and several types of sparrows. Once, I even saw a woodpecker near the feeder. He was probably enjoying the company of so many birds. I found that my red friend was a finch, and I was still waiting for her.

Soon, birds were fighting because the feeder was too small for so many. We decided to make more feeders. Before long, five feeders were in our garden. One we hung right under the roof outside my window. Soon, a bird chorus was singing in the garden every day They arrived at various times throughout the day. Some came in groups, some alone. One group, for instance, was chickadees, and I called them mini birds. They fly everywhere in a group; they eat quickly and quickly fly away. It astonished me how they are so tiny and cute.

The feeder in front of my window was empty for a long time. I was thinking about moving it to the garden because I thought that perhaps birds did not like to come too close to the house. But, one sunny day, I was looking outside as she appeared. My red friend was sitting in the feeder just outside my window. She was hovering around and looking at me. After a while, the beauty took a seed and flew away. I stayed watching the feeder and soon there were seven more. She brought seven red finches. I was in a dream world. They were observing all parts of the feeder and looking in my room and at me. The birds were not scared. I was fascinated and could not move. Then they left the feeder but returned the next day. From that day and until now, they visit my feeder, but not regularly.

I never know when their majesties will visit me again. Sometimes I don't see them for days. When they are away, I imagine that they are traveling somewhere, maybe seeing new cities, eating new seeds, and making new friends. But I know that someday they will return. I always wait for them with plenty of their favorite treats in the feeder.

Birds were my first friends in America, and they formed my first impressions about the country. After the happy experience with the birds, everything that is American seemed great and wonderful. Now I love American people, food, restaurants, and music. I have many new friends, but the most precious of them are my birds.

## Amazing
HEYDY ANTEZANA

ᴍy FAMILY CAME TO THE USA from Bolivia two and a half years ago. My husband has a three-year work visa and will probably extend that for another three years. So, we are not really immigrants, but we expect to stay in the United States for several years. Our kids go to school, my husband goes to work, and I go to college to study English.

The first year we lived in Hayward, California. My husband worked all day, and I stayed at home with my children because it was summer vacation and I didn't drive. I also didn't have friends or family. I felt alone in the beginning and found this new life very hard. After three months, school started, and my kids went to a Christian school in Union City, and I went to adult school to learn English. My husband told me about ESL classes at Chabot College and encouraged me to go there, which I did for a short time. I didn't complete the program because we moved to Pleasanton. We decided to move to Pleasanton because we learned that the schools are excellent. We wanted a better environment for our children. My children started classes at Mohr Elementary School and at the YMCA program; my husband enjoys his work, and I am enrolled in ESL classes at Las Positas College.

Our lives have settled into a comfortable place in our temporary home, with new friends and new appreciation. The move to America has changed my life in several different ways. I have discovered new qualities in myself, and I have a different way of understanding new situations. I often smile and think, "I did it," I feel more mentally and physically strong. Starting a new life is hard, but the experience is amazing.

## Becoming Independent

ANONYMOUS

*M*OST PEOPLE HAVE MANY PROBLEMS when they first move to another country. International students especially have a lot of problems. I am an international student, and I just came to the USA a few months ago. Since coming here, I have had many problems, such as finding housing, learning to drive a car, speaking English, understanding what people say, living alone, making foreign friends, and getting good grades in my class. Everything is new and difficult for me. However, speaking English, driving a car, and living alone are the most difficult.

Speaking English is one of the most difficult things I have encountered since I came to the United States. I could say, "Hello," and "Nice to meet you." But I couldn't say anything else, so I have had lots of problems. For example, in the classroom, the teacher asked me some questions, but I could not respond. I tried to say something, but while I was thinking of an answer and how to say it in English, the teacher was already looking for someone else to answer the question. I felt uncomfortable because the teacher might have thought I was either very shy or a very bad student. I am neither; I just could not speak English very well. My classmates might also have thought the same thing, which also made me depressed. I became so tense that I could not make myself speak English at all. This has been a major problem.

One day, I met an American friend, a policeman in San Francisco. This friendship has been very comforting for me because we can have casual conversations. Unfortunately, even causal conversations do not always go well. In one conversation, he asked me what I had done the day before. My response was not perfect because I was tense. I said, "I did head cut." I wanted to say, "I got a hair cut." But it didn't come out well. He was really surprised and worried about my head. He asked questions about how I had cut my head. Can you imagine that? I then had to quickly say that my head was not cut; my hair was cut. It was a very stressful experience.

Driving on California freeways and on busy streets is another difficult thing for me. I had a bad experience regarding this a few months ago. I was driving home from Las Positas when I got a ticket. This is what happened. I slowed down as I approached a red light and looked both left and right for on-coming cars. When I didn't see any cars, I turned right. Immediately, I saw red lights flashing in my rear view mirror, and when I pulled over, the policeman gave me a ticket. I really did not understand the reason for the ticket, so I felt a little angry. As politely as possible, I asked the policeman to explain the reason for the ticket. He said that I did not stop at the red light. He explained that I had to stop completely before turning. I had almost stopped, which is perfectly fine in my country because my speed was less than ten miles an hour. However, the policeman did not accept my reason for not stopping, and he gave me a ticket. This is a cultural difference, not really an illegal stop. This misunderstanding cost me three hundred and fifty dollars. It made me sad and crazy.

An additional point about driving is the one-way streets. In my country, there are very few one-way streets, but in America there are many, and there are many lanes depending on the street. Often, the sign for a one-way street is very small. So these streets are difficult to use correctly. I never actually drove the wrong way, but I almost did on many occasions.

Living alone is most difficult for me. I had never lived alone before I came to the United States. That means I did not have any experience with living alone. I didn't know what I had to do in daily life. I had many problems and felt homesick. I missed my friends and family and felt frustrated and sad because I couldn't see them. The feelings were difficult to overcome because I was really alone. Preparing meals was especially difficult because I had never cooked before I came to the USA. I went out to eat for almost every meal, so I spent all of my money on eating out. Poverty was also a new experience. One month I spent all of my money before the middle of the month, so I had no food for over a week. This experience motivated me to learn to cook.

In conclusion, there were many difficult things when I first came to America. The language problems are still difficult, but now I am a good driver and a pretty good cook. I learned from my mistakes and have become independent. I am confident that I will overcome the difficulties of living in the USA because I hope to graduate from an American university and perhaps even find a job in the United States. I pray for good luck.

CHAPTER FOUR
# Then and Now

The Old Country and the New

Remembrances of My Family

Perseverance Pays

Unexpected Future

The Kindness of Others

My Opinions

A New Person

With New Eyes

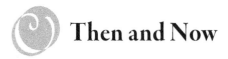 # Then and Now

## The Old Country and the New

MARILYN MARQUIS

*M*Y MOTHER'S FAMILY EMIGRATED FROM Italy in 1903. That is the beginning of our family's story in the United States. My grandparents grew up in a small town in Italy, fell in love, and moved to America after they were married on Saint Joseph's Day, March 19, 1902, which my mother always thought gave her family a unique connection to the Holy Family, Jesus, Mary, and Joseph, and connected them to their religion in a special way. They moved to a small town in New York in 1903, had thirteen children, and eventually moved to Chicago. At the time they arrived on Ellis Island for immigration processing, the typical process included a name change. So the Rosati family name was changed to Ross.

My mother, the eighth child, spoke only Italian until she started elementary school, but as the family grew and the older children were established in their social lives and school, English became the language of home. None of her sisters and brothers spoke Italian as adults. This was a fairly typical experience of immigrant families at the time.

When I was growing up in California, a typical question children asked each other was, "What are you?" which meant, "What nationality is your family?" The combinations were always interesting: half Italian, one quarter Irish, one quarter we don't really know; half German and half Irish; half French and half Swedish. Very few students at my school were one hundred percent anything, but we all knew where our families came from and felt unique because of that combined connection to "The Old Country."

The other thing that made me feel special as a child was having more cousins than any other person I ever met, over 30 first cousins just from my mother's family. There are now over one hundred and seventy descendants from Donato Antonio Rosati and Elizabeth Ruggieri. One of my cousins keeps a record of marriages, births, and deaths so we can always contact each other and stay connected with our family's growth. I often imagine how proud our grandparents would be to see the efforts that are made to keep our heritage alive. Several of my cousins have even changed their names from Ross back to Rosati to keep the connection alive. Additionally, the family holds a Ross Family picnic on the fourth of July every year to celebrate not only Independence Day but also our grandparents' coming to America.

When I was a child, I enjoyed hearing stories of my mother's childhood. I was fascinated by the prospect of having nine sisters and three brothers and wondered how they all ate dinner together and what the house was like. Where did they all sleep? I especially loved hearing my mother sing in Italian. She did not remember much Italian for speaking, but she could sing lots of songs for us.

My mother always spoke fondly of her mother's English teacher. Grandma worked very hard to learn the language of her children and grandchildren, but it was never easy. In those days there were no ESL programs at adult school or community college, so Grandma had a teacher who came to her house. They would sit in the parlor where only the priest and the English teacher were allowed. My mother described how the teacher wore all black, including a black veil, widow's clothes, and at the end of the lesson, she would sip sherry through her veil. Perhaps the stories about those English lessons gave me an early understanding both of how important it is for immigrants to learn English, and of how difficult it is.

As I got older and had children of my own, the importance of keeping family history alive became more significant. My sister and I asked our mother to write down some memories of her childhood, but she couldn't imagine how those memories would be important. I regret that I did not take a more active part in recording her family history. After my mother died in 2008, I found some of her memories written in a spiral notebook. She never told us that she had begun to write about her life, so it was a lovely surprise when we found the notebook among her things.

As you read her memories, imagine your family one hundred years in the future. What will the collective memory of your children and grandchildren be? I hope this short passage of my mother's childhood memories will inspire you to write those things you want to share with your future relatives.

# Remembrances of My Family

OLGA MARQUIS

*I* HAVE HEARD SO MANY STORIES about my father and mother from other members of our family that my children feel I should tell some of my memories. They may differ from some of my family's remembrances, but that is understandable.

Both of my parents were born in Roccamorice, Abruzzo, Italy. I do not know what year my father first came to America. He could have been here a couple of years or more. He established himself and returned to Italy and married my mother. They returned to America, settling in Geneva, New York. They were married March 19, 1902. Helen was their first child, born on February 29, 1904.

They lived in an apartment on Exchange Street, in Geneva, New York. I recall them saying there was a fire there, so they had to move. Where to, I don't know. They eventually moved to 34 Lewis Street. I believe Jule was the first one born there. Most of the Italians who settled in Geneva lived in a section called Torey Park. Pa said "No way. I came to America; I'll live with the Americans." For neighbors, we had Irish, Germans, and English.

Mother got enough money together to put a down payment on the house. They probably paid about two thousand dollars for it. We lived in the house until we moved to Chicago in 1926.

My father had a shoe repair shop on Exchange Street. His specialty was making shoes for people with clubfeet. He had one woman, I recall, with one leg shorter than the other by about 10 inches. Pa built up the shoe by placing one thin sole after another until she walked no longer with a limp. The nuns at our school had beautiful high top boots, as did my mother, which my father made. Pa took care of their repair work, too. He could mend a hole in the leather where you couldn't tell where it was. Evidently the Rosati's all learned the trade from their father, as I know dad's brothers, Frank and Louis, were shoe repairmen as well.

My father loved music. He knew many of the arias and popular Italian songs. He sang while he worked, and many a time you would find people standing outside his shop listening to him sing. We had a record player, and when he could, he would buy records. Caruso was his favorite tenor. In Italy, when he was a young man, everyone was obligated to serve in the army. I don't know for how long. Anyway, dad played the horn and the tuba in the army and continued to enjoy playing. Every Sunday morning he would play his instruments in the back yard. I know he drove the neighbors wild, but that was his way of relaxing.

Pa had wine with all of his meals. Ma never drank, but once a year she made dandelion wine for Pa. Pa's specialty was making cordials. These we were allowed. In our back yard we had a grape arbor, probably about 10 x 15 feet with a table and benches — homemade of course. In the summertime we spent hours there, out of the sun. I loved to cut out paper dolls there. It was a great time. We were not supposed to touch the grapes, as Pa wanted them to make wine. However, by the time he got around to checking their ripeness, they were practically all gone.

Shrove Tuesday, the Tuesday night before Ash Wednesday, was a big night. We had family and friends in, and there was much dancing. My father tried to teach us the tarantella. He was very light on his feet. Another thing I remember about Shrove Tuesday is the older ones would dress up like they do in New Orleans, as it was carnival night. I only remember Jule dressed in my father's pants and shirt with a pillow stuck in the front.

I also recall Pa sitting on the floor; he would put first one leg, then the other over his shoulders. He did another maneuver where he was on all fours. He could move his right leg all around by lifting his hands each time he brought the leg around. I've tried, but to no avail.

Preparing food for a large family took a great deal of time in those days. Most people grew at least some of their food. We had a nice big yard where we raised vegetables, peaches and pears, and chickens. The chicken yard was fenced in and there was a chicken coop. When we killed a chicken, Ma would drown it in boiling water. Then we had to pluck the feathers off. Children always had a part to play in food preparation. Friday was bread day. I don't know how many loaves of bread Ma made. We would come in from school and she would hand us a piece of fresh baked bread with olive oil on it. She also made a lot of her spaghetti. I can still see her rolling out the dough, then folding it so she could cut it in the thin strips. If I tried that I'm sure I would cut my fingers off.

My dad loved polenta. On Friday nights he came in late from work. Ma would sauté garlic and pour it over his polenta. Then he would take a dried hot pepper and break it over the top. One thing we always had was small hot peppers hung on a string. When you wanted one, you just yanked it off the string.

My mother kept a trunk full of beautiful material that she purchased at the dry goods store in town. Our dresses were made of wool, crepe de chine, satin, and silk. You name it; she could make it. All the clothes were made without a pattern. Don't ask me how she did it. She loved to sew and did a lot of it. I can remember going to school in a new dress and the teacher would send me to the other teachers to show it off. The dresses she made for the older girls were all in the latest style. She really had a flair for clothes. Ma made my wedding dress and complete trousseau. My dresses were really beautiful. My granddaughter, Michelle, wore my wedding dress when she and Joe were married.

My godfather lived in Philadelphia. One year he sent us a baby lamb. He was our pet; we treated it like you would a dog. When it grew up, we used to ride it around the backyard. When Pa decided it was time to have it butchered, he took it to the Armor Company. Needless to say none of us would have any part of it. We were all mad at Pa. Even as an adult so many years later, I rarely eat lamb and never cooked it myself when I was raising my own children.

17 min

## Perseverance Pays

ADRIAN RANGEL

LIVING IN THE UNITED STATES OF AMERICA has been the most wonderful experience in my life because I have learned how to take care of myself without my parents' help. Gaining personal independence was a major goal when first I came here. I had a strong need to prove that I could take care of myself. My first effort was to find a stable job and to earn my own money. I found different kinds of jobs; I was a dishwasher first, then a pre-cook, and finally a cook. I also learned how to drive a car, and was on my way to real independence.

My first job was at the Sweet River Saloon, an American restaurant in Pleasanton, CA. My friend, Ricardo, was the cook at that restaurant and suggested that I apply for a job there as a dishwasher. He stopped by my house one night after work and said that he would introduce me to the manager the next day. Naturally, I was appreciative and happy. I had been waiting for an opportunity like this. Ricardo was convinced that the manager would give me a work schedule immediately. However, I remember that night I didn't sleep well in anticipation of my first job. I thought about how unfamiliar the job would be. After tossing and turning, I finally fell asleep. The next morning, Ricardo woke me up at 7 AM with a phone call. I got up, took a shower, and I went with him to my new job. He introduced me to the manager, who was waiting for us and did indeed offer me the job. After a short interview with my good friend translating for us, the manager said, "The job is yours. I hope you do well." I was surprised to learn that I would start working immediately. I went to the dishwasher area and saw a lot of dishes waiting for me. I took a deep breath and said to myself, "Come on, Adrian, you can do it." I made the decision and started to clean all the dishes on the table. I had no experience washing dishes, but I learned quickly.

Language proved to be the most difficult aspect of life in the USA. I didn't even know how to say hi to the other employees on my first day of work. After the first day, the other days were a piece of cake. Then after I knew that I could deal with this job, I took some English classes at El Caminito School in Livermore. Studying English helped me in my job because I could understand more when I spoke with my manager and co-workers. After four months as a dishwasher, I was promoted to pre-cook. It was an amusing moment because when my manager offered me that position, I didn't really understand everything that he said. I realized that I should say, "Yes," but it took me a moment to realize that he had just offered me a promotion and a raise in pay. I remember feeling very proud of myself. I spent three months as a pre-cook and then had another opportunity. One of the cooks decided to move to another state and again my manager offered me the position. I accepted, of course. This time he gave me an even better raise. I was very happy because, from the time I started working at this restaurant, this was my goal.

My second step to independence was driving. When I started working, I had to take the bus, which was not easy because of my limited English. My friend, Ricardo, taught me how to use the bus and gave me the bus numbers that I needed to get to and from work, but I really wanted to buy my own car and learn to drive in California. In Mexico, I drove some, but the rules and driving conditions are very different. Eventually, I bought a 1990 Ford Escort. It was a little bit old, but it was in good condition. One problem was that in Mexico I learned to drive an automatic, but the Escort had a standard transmission. A friend taught me how to drive the stick shift, and when I learned how to drive my car, I felt like the most important guy in the world. The next step was studying for the driving test. I prepared very well and finally went to the DMV. Then they gave me my first driver license in California. I have had this license for five years.

My first experiences in the United States were sometimes difficult and sometimes scary, but these experiences taught me how to be better every single day and to never give up. I learned that perseverance and hard work lead to success.

# Unexpected Future

NAOKO VIOLETTE

*A*T ONE TIME IN MY life, I couldn't have imagined myself living in the USA or any foreign country. I thought I would live in Japan forever because I wasn't interested in foreign countries, and, as a high school student, the world outside of Japan was unrealistic for me. But, a reluctant decision changed all that.

In my last year of high school, I had to decide what to do after graduation. I didn't know what I wanted to do in the future, but my one dream was to experience living by myself in a big city like Tokyo. I grew up in the countryside of Japan, so the big city seemed exciting. My parents supported my going to college in a big city because of the better job opportunities after graduation, but they didn't support going to the big city to have fun. One day, they suggested that I study English abroad. This was a surprise because we all knew that I wasn't good at English. When I heard this idea, I really didn't like it because I didn't want to be apart from my friends. I tried to come up with some good reasons that this was not such a good idea and told them to my parents to convince them that I should go to college in Japan. They were not convinced. I still couldn't decide what I wanted to do, so my parents made arrangements for me to go to Canada, and I reluctantly agreed.

My parents found an agency which arranged for me to attend a private ESL school in Vancouver and stay with a Canadian family. My English level was unbelievably low, so I had difficulty communicating with my host family and I had to start school in the very beginning class. My early experiences were not very happy. Even though the Canadian family was very nice to me, I wanted to go home, badly. I missed my parents and friends and felt angry at my parents for sending a teenage girl alone to a foreign country. I had never even lived outside my hometown before. Sadly, I knew what I would do if I went back to Japan: nothing. You see, I struggled with many different emotions, and through it all, I frantically studied to survive. After a few months, I had made a lot of friends from school, and my English level quickly improved, so I was comfortable living there. Many of my friends lived downtown, where my school was located, and it was inconvenient to commute to school from my host family's house, so I decided to rent my very first apartment downtown. I had a wonderful time with my friends and teachers, but also I wanted to make friends who were native English speakers to help improve my English. One of my Japanese friends had two really good friends, one Canadian and one American. He arranged for me and my friend to meet the two of them. I had a good time with them even though it was difficult to understand them. From then on, I often hung out with them, especially with the American, and later I started to date him. At the time, I had already been in Vancouver for six months, and very soon my parents wanted me to assess my English by taking a college entrance exam in Japan. So I went back to Japan for two weeks and then returned to Vancouver. My time in Vancouver was so pleasant that I no longer wanted to go back to Japan. But a few months later my parents called me and said that I passed the college entrance test and that I should come back to Japan in two months to go to college. Once again, I tried to change their mind, but once again, it didn't work. I returned to Japan to go to college and continued to study English there.

When I started college in Japan, I was mad at my parents again. Even though my previous dream of living by myself in a big city in Japan came true, I was unhappy. I thought a lot about quitting college and going back to Canada, but I didn't have any money without my parents' help. I unwillingly stuck with the school. My American boyfriend and I still had a relationship, and a year later when he graduated, he came to Japan and lived with me. I was really surprised that my parents permitted us to live together because I thought they were really rather old-fashioned. I am glad they were not. After I graduated from college, we got married, and we both worked for about three and a half years in Japan. At the time, we often took short trips to different parts of Asia since I had become interested in foreign countries. We had a good life. One day, his parents called him and asked if we would come and help with their business in the United States. We both liked living in Japan, but we weren't sure that we wanted to continue our jobs permanently, so we decided to accept their offer. We also decided to travel around the world for six months before we settled in the USA. This had long been a dream of ours, and it seemed like a good time to do it. We traveled through Asia, the Middle East, and Europe, about thirty countries in all. After traveling, we settled in the United States, and I've been studying English for a year and a half now.

I wasn't interested in foreign countries in my youth, but because my parents insisted that I go to Canada, my attitude has changed. Living in the USA was an unexpected future for me, and I realize that if I hadn't gone to Canada, my life would be very different. I now really appreciate that my parents encouraged me to have these valuable experiences. If not for my parents, I couldn't have met all those precious people, who are still good friends of mine. I don't know where I will be in a few years, but now I enjoy where I am.

HUA ZHOU

WITH VERY LITTLE PREPARATION, MY daughter and I came to America from China on September 18, 1999, because my husband was hired by a small business. He moved three months before our arrival, so we were eager to see him again. When we first arrived, we lived in hardship, for we lacked knowledge of the American lifestyle, and we didn't speak English.

After being in the United States for one month, we had a big surprise. I was pregnant. We didn't have health insurance because we did not know about it when we arrived in the USA. My husband's company only bought health insurance for him, not for my daughter or me. Also, we discovered that the company paid my husband only half the salary of others who had similar positions. His salary was just enough to meet our living needs. Without insurance and without extra money, my daughter could not even see a doctor when she was sick. Once she had a high fever and a stomach ache for several days. She curled up on an old sofa, held her stomach, and cried. My husband and I watched her suffering but could do nothing for her except comfort her. My heart was bleeding. Also, without health insurance, I couldn't get any pregnancy exams. I kept calling insurance agents hoping to buy health insurance for my daughter and me, but the insurance companies refused to insure us since I was pregnant.

Besides insurance, we had language problems. At first, I hardly understood any English. One day, my husband turned on the radio in his car when he drove us to the store. After listening for about ten minutes, I finally understood the word "Safeway" because the person on the radio kept saying that word over and over. Additionally, nobody could understand what I said because of my heavy accent and bad grammar. Language issues prevented me from getting help from any organizations or other kind people. My husband was busy at his new job, but he also suffered language problems since he had never studied English in America. I felt as if I was living on a desolate island. Without health insurance, without communication skills, without friends, and without relatives, we lived in America with unimaginable difficulty.

Fortunately, we lived in a great city, Pleasanton, California. We eventually got help from people whom we had not known before. Two Chinese ladies who work in the Pleasanton library assisted me during my hardest times. One of them, named Linda, told me how to register at the library to get free one-on-one language assistance. Another one, named Yu, called nonprofit corporations for me to ask for help with health insurance. After a few weeks, I was assigned an English teacher who was seeking teaching experience. She talked to me two hours every week for several months. Furthermore, one of the companies which Yu called told her that we needed to pay $2,000 total for me and the baby during the time I was in the hospital. The cost was originally more than $10,000. All of the help soothed my heart and comforted my anxieties.

In addition to getting help from people around us, my husband got assistance from his co-workers, too. Before he arrived in America, my husband had been asked to sign a contract which stated that he would work in the same company for three years. After working several months, my husband was told by nice co-workers that the contract he had signed was illegal, so he quit his first job and found a much better job at a bigger company located in San

Francisco. This company bought health insurance not only for my husband, but also for my daughter and me. Moreover, this business paid him the salary that he deserved. From then on, our hardship of living in the USA was over.

## My Opinions

ANONYMOUS

*O*NCE I DECIDED TO STUDY in the United States, everything went very fast, and before I realized it, I was already sitting in a plane heading toward the USA. It seems like it was yesterday, but it has actually already been one and a half years since I stepped into the United States for the first time. You may think that it is not a very long time ago, but I believe it has been long enough for me to find out what is going on here. My opinion about Americans and the USA has changed several times, and I would like to share some of those opinions.

My first opinion was that America is the best place in the universe. After my arrival, I felt like I came into a completely different world where everything was new and exciting. First, I was surprised that I understood everything pretty well and surprised that native speakers got the idea of what I was saying, too. Furthermore, I was proud of living in the same country as my favorite Hollywood stars and musicians. I just loved everything, the huge freeways, the nice people, my new school, the service in the stores, and mainly San Francisco. When I went there for the first time, I was amazed like a kid who got her first bike.

Shortly after my first opinion came the opinion that America is the worst place ever. I know it seems like a huge jump, but believe me, there wasn't any time in between. I suddenly realized that I had no idea what Americans were saying and that I actually didn't understand them at all. I stopped going to sandwich places because I simply did not understand the staff, and that led to getting exactly the opposite of what I actually wanted. Gradually, it got even worse. I'm not an alcoholic or a big drinker, but I wondered why I could not drink any alcohol in the United States when I was already twenty, and I had already been drinking in the Czech Republic for two years before I came here. I began to think that many things about America were not what they seemed to be at first. The huge freeways became big noisy traffic jams, the nice people became people I could not communicate with, and school was just a lot of work. The store clerk's inquiries became annoying questions. "Do you need help with your groceries?" or "Can I help you find something?" became irritating challenges. Finally, even San Francisco became boring. Furthermore, I realized that there was absolutely no possibility of seeing my favorite actors or musicians roaming freely in the city. In addition to all these negatives, the worst one came; I started to miss my home, my family, my boyfriend, and all of my friends.

It was hard to get over my second opinion, but then eventually my opinion neutralized. I found out that everywhere is pretty much the same. There are positive and negative things everywhere, in my country and in America too. I realized that it doesn't matter where I am and that I will have good days and bad days over here as I did in the Czech Republic. I started to look at everything from both sides and not look only at the negatives anymore which helped me to face up to reality.

If you have just arrived in the USA, prepare yourself for ups and downs. There will most likely be moments when you will love it here, and there will be other moments when you will hate it. I have experienced both, and still the only thing I suggest is to just stay patient and don't give up.

## A New Person
ANONYMOUS

*I* HAVE BEEN LIVING IN THE USA for twenty-one months, each of them unique, each including good and bad. I come from a third world country with a different mindset, culture, language, and social environment. For me, adapting to the life in a foreign country has included discovering and accepting.

A new place means encountering many new situations and people. The visual impact was stunning at first. Everything looked totally different, the people, the food, the buildings, the roads, the plants and trees, everything. The sounds were different, too. For example, I had never met anyone from Thailand, nor had I heard anyone speaking Farsi. To me every moment was an opportunity to discover new things that I had never experienced before.

America is very different from my native country. For instance, it is hard to come from a country where 81% of the population lives on less than a dollar a day. In contrast, here I see people waste resources at home, in restaurants, in offices, and in factories. It is not something that will change anytime soon, nor is it America's fault. It hurts to see how people waste resources that would make a huge difference in other parts of the world. When I first went to a restaurant,

I was amazed at how much food they serve, and at the same time, how much food they just throw away. It is difficult to get used to the American size of portions. Anyone who has not been here before is shocked to see what a Big Gulp is.

My experiences in the USA have been both great and not so great, just like any other place in the world. One of the best memories I have is spending a lot of time at one of the best universities in the world, UC Berkeley. Being in the very same place where Nobel Prize winners teach and having the opportunity to listen to some lectures every once in a while is something that, thanks to a friend of mine, I will never forget. At the same time, I discovered how many opportunities exist for anyone willing to try. No wonder this is called the land of opportunities. Education is the key to success, and it can be easily found here.

I am sure anyone can recall great memories as well as bad experiences when trying to adapt to a new life in a foreign country. My life has definitely changed in the last months and no matter where I am in the next five years, I will always remember how I came from a different country and turned myself into a new person.

## With New Eyes
DARLYNSON LIRA

*I* FIRST ARRIVED IN THE USA approximately two years ago. I came from Brazil to visit relatives and to discover a different culture. I had traveled throughout Europe teaching the essence of Brazilian Jiu-Jitsu martial arts for eight months before coming to the United States, and I felt especially enthusiastic about coming here for the first time. Everything felt fresh and adventurous. My first impression was that everything here relied on three things: organization, respect, and security. I eventually decided to stay in the USA because I wanted to advance my career in the fitness field, and I realized this was the right place to reach my career goals.

The experience I have gained by living in the USA has altered my thinking in both positive and negative ways. I was eager to understand how things work out in American culture, things such as peoples' behavior, ways of living, and the job market. I found that living here brought me a greater sense of security than I had in comparison to my home country. In Brazil, for example, if you left your car open, you would probably never see it again, or all the parts would have been taken or broken. The lack of security has always been part of Brazilian life, but here things are different. Many times I have left my car unlocked when shopping for groceries. Once when I realized my car was left in a parking lot with the door unlocked, I ran back to the parking lot to lock the door and found that the car was safe. A sense of relief overwhelmed me as I contrasted this experience to those I had had in Brazil. Nothing has happened to my property since I moved to this blessed country.

Work-wise, the opportunities to improve my career and gain larger recognition for what I do for a living have been a highlight of my experience in this country. Jiu-Jitsu has become very popular and even overrated in Brazil, and many new academies have opened in recent years because of that popularity. However, because of the growth of the business, competition for students has changed the way businesses are operated. In the USA, I found it easier to earn a living with my martial arts background since not too many academies are located in one single neighborhood, unlike the current situation in Brazil. Also, people here seem more respectful of the profession; they give it more value and recognize it not just as a fighting tool, but also as a sport. Living in the USA has given me enough strength to think positively and to increase success in my career.

Even with all the positive aspects of my experience here, living in a foreign country makes me feel homesick most of the time. I miss my family and friends; I miss the weather and the entertaining lifestyle; I miss the Brazilian way. Most of my family is back in Brazil: my father, my mother, my brothers, my students, my childhood friends. The people whom I've known for many years are now very far from me. Not having those whom I love and care for around me gives me a sense of loneliness and hardship. However, I am constantly contacting them, so I feel less alone. I have also found it difficult to get accustomed to the weather. I miss the heat and humidity from my country. I am not used to very low temperatures. Even when I go out at night during spring and summer, the temperatures are still too cold for me. My skin has become drier, and I have to apply lotion most of the time in order to hydrate what the weather here destroys.

The lifestyle here, especially the nightlife, is also very different from Brazil. People here get all dressed up to go to a nightclub, but the evening lasts just three hours. The clubs start turning the lights out before 2 AM, just as the party is getting exciting. Definitely, Brazilians know how to party, and we can rock all night until 6 AM the next morning. People work hard throughout the week and get the most out of the fabulous beaches and exciting night life on weekends. Additionally, carnival season in Brazil is famous for all-night partying, but here the only carnival party offered is in the heart of San Francisco with a mix of cultures in foggy weather.

It just is not the same. I suppose that there are things about Brazil that I will always miss.

Living in the United States, though, has provided invaluable experience and surpassed all of my expectations. I see things with different eyes. Before coming to this country, I did not know how I would overcome the cultural obstacles, such as language and lifestyle, but I have. Although I miss my family and the fun life of my home country, I now understand and admire a lot of things that have come to be part of my life in this country. I am proud to say that I was able to acquire, not just more experience, but also a new language, new friends, an open door for my career, and a new life.

CHAPTER FIVE

# Differences

 # Differences

## Regional Differences

MARILYN MARQUIS

*U*NLIKE ALL OF THE OTHER contributors to this volume, I have never lived outside my home country, the United States. I have traveled to Europe, Asia, and North America, but I have only lived in my native country and in my native language. My understanding of differences comes from traveling, living in several different states in the United States, and from listening to my students who come from every corner of the world.

I was raised in southern California and lived there most of my life. As I grew up, I thought that the whole country, perhaps the whole world, was like southern California with blue skies, warm weather, beautiful beaches, majestic mountains, and of course Disneyland and movie stars. I was very surprised when, after I was married, I moved to Kentucky, then Texas, Alabama, and New Mexico and discovered that language is only one small difference when we consider all of what makes up culture. When I first lived in Kentucky, I was acutely aware of the smell of the city. It rained in the summer, a most shocking surprise, so the plants and flowers are different and so are the smells. Humid air is heavy, so smells linger. I was accustomed to the afternoon breeze off the ocean that ensures fresh air and fresh smells.

The United States is a big country, so it is not surprising that people and customs in different parts of the country differ significantly. If you look at the cookbooks in a library or bookstore, you will see books about the many regional differences in food, differences in the choice of vegetables and meat as well as in the methods of preparation. This is true for different regions in Italy, France, Mexico and probably most countries of the world. When my students write about food, however, it becomes very clear that when newcomers first arrive in the United States and see highways lined with fast food chains, they assume that American cooking is hamburgers and French fries or fried chicken. They seem skeptical when I say that I never cook hamburgers at home or that I rarely eat at fast food chains.

When I lived in Alabama, I was astonished by the beautiful gardens, especially the azaleas in spring. The gardens seemed natural, much less manicured than the gardens in southern California. I had never seen such green nature. Ivy-covered trees lined the country roads, no freeways in rural Alabama. Rivers and streams dissect the state. In addition to the lush landscape, I was surprised not to find tracts of uniform houses, which is the norm in southern California and much of northern California. Instead I saw small houses next door to very large houses. Nothing seemed to match. California has strict zoning laws which require a permit for building. The building codes also limit what kind of structures can be next to each other. California looks the way it does because most of the buildings are post 1950. Alabama has a very different and much longer history. Every region in the United States has a unique style, so the houses and buildings look quite different from California.

When I first moved away from home, I wrote letters to my family and friends (this was before the Internet), describing how I felt as if I were in a different country. Nothing was familiar, not even attitudes about what is attractive or what is socially acceptable. Of course, those differences are not as dramatic as those from country to country, but they seemed very significant to me.

## Return Policy
### YUKIKO EGAWA

IN THE UNITED STATES, PEOPLE can return anything within a certain time period if they have the receipt, regardless of the reasons. When you change your mind, or your kids don't like the clothes you bought, or you don't like the taste of something, just grab the receipt and take the item back to the customer service counter of the store. You'll be able to get a refund easily. There is often a long line in front of the customer service, but the system is easy and good for consumers.

The return policy works for gifts as well. When you purchase a birthday gift, for example, the clerk will ask if you want a gift receipt. If you receive a gift, you may also see a gift receipt in the box. This allows the recipient of that gift to return the gift easily. If you get a gift you don't like or want, you can take it back. Then you can get what you really want instead.

The return policy is really amazing. Once I even saw a woman return a half-eaten birthday cake at a big warehouse store. I was surprised because she had already used the cake for the birthday party and had eaten half of it. She said that she didn't like the taste, and she got a refund. Apparently, some people use this easy return system selfishly, just for their own advantage. That is the risk of this free society.

Because of this return culture, there are a lot of items in every store that appear to be used. Especially in the sale items, you can often find slightly dirty clothes or shoes, which someone has already worn outside of the store. Once I saw a woman return a lipstick to the store, so I don't buy cosmetics without checking the item inside the box. I can't trust whether everything sold in stores is new. Here in the United States, we can return items easily, but at the same time we have to shop more carefully.

In contrast, in Japan we can't easily return the items that we have bought. The attitude is very different. Consumers make a choice to purchase something and have to accept responsibility for that decision. Consequently, before shoppers make a purchase, they think about it more carefully and decide if it is really worth it. Stores don't have to accept returned items unless there is a defect. Returning something is considered morally wrong. Of course, customers can exchange the items for another size or color, but usually they can't get a refund.

Now my shopping habits have changed, and I shop like an American. If I see something attractive, I buy it without thinking so much, and then when I go back to my house, I decide if I want to keep it or not. If I go back to Japan, I will have to be more careful when I go shopping.

*A*RRANGED MARRIAGE HAS LONG ROOTS in the history of many countries and is still practiced in many parts of the world, such as Afghanistan, Pakistan, India, and other parts of Asia. Many people trust in arranged marriage and feel confident about the commitments they make. The western world does not practice arranged marriage, so when I came to the United States, I encountered a very different method for finding a spouse. In many countries, parents prefer to arrange the marriages of their children because marriage is a life-long commitment and requires a lot of consideration.

In the western world like the United States, children learn at a young age to be educated, self-confident, and active making life decisions. Teenagers have freedom to work outside the home where they meet other young people and develop independent friendships. Young men and women also have many opportunities to get to know each other over a long period of time before making a marriage decision. If they make a poor decision, they have the opportunity of marrying again with the blessing of their families.

Arranged marriage is common in Afghan society. Parents want someone suitable for their whole family, and they do not want their son or daughter to marry outside of the family's circle of friends and relatives. Young men and women do not even have the opportunity to know each other before the engagement or wedding. As a result, the parents feel obligated to find a good match for their children. Parents look for a good spouse, someone who will take care of them when they get older. They want someone they know, such as a relative or friend.

My marriage is an example of this kind of marriage. Our marriage was arranged by my husband's parents. His family is related to mine. My husband was already living in the United States attending medical college when the marriage arrangements were made. He had completed an engineering degree at a university in Kabul, Afghanistan, but left the country for political reasons. His parents did not want him to marry someone they did not know, so they began the search for a good match. They chose me, and without my knowledge, they began to talk to my parents. Since they knew each other, they were very happy to make the match. No one ever asked me my thoughts about the marriage. After they made the decision and the engagement was confirmed, they sent me out of the country. First, I went to Pakistan and then to Germany. I waited for two and a half years before I received a visa to come to the United States.

I have been married for twenty-three years. Through these years, I have had many happy days and, of course, some sad days, too. All marriages have ups and downs. My generation and my children's generation have very different ideas about marriage. My children grew up in a different culture from mine. I will give my opinion to them when they are ready to make decisions about their lives. I want to help them make the right choices. Arranged marriage is not always ideal, but for me it brought a happy life.

# The Presidential Election

YOJIRO SUDO

THE UNITED STATES PRESIDENTIAL ELECTION comes every four years, and many famous presidents have been elected, such as John F. Kennedy and Abraham Lincoln. In November 2008, I had the remarkable experience of seeing the first African American president elected in the United States. His name is Barack Obama. Although I will experience many amazing events in my life, I think this event will remain the most significant event for me.

I felt that most Americans believed they could change the government with their vote. During the presidential election, Barack Obama repeated and repeated, "Yes, we can." "Yes, we can." It means people who live in America can change the nation. Many Americans have trusted his words, and some people have taken action. In contrast, in Japan, my native country, most people do not believe that they can change the complicated system of government. We think that the government doesn't belong to the people, so most people, especially the younger generation, aren't interested in the government.

Electing the first African American president was a very important event in American history. This presidential election will be discussed not only by Americans, but also by people around the globe for a long time. And because I was present at the time, I can discuss what happened on that day from my personal experience.

The election of the first African American president demonstrates to everyone that now a person from any nationality has the opportunity to be elected president of the United States. Twenty years ago no one could have imagined an African American president. Now, however, we can imagine an Asian American or a Mexican American president being elected in the future.

The presidential election of 2008 was a significant event for me. I will explain this important event to my next generation, and that generation will tell the next, spreading the story over many generations. Because of this election, I imagine a world where nothing is impossible. If we trust, persevere, and exert an effort, we can achieve anything. American people believe they could change the nation, and they will achieve their goal. The Japanese government needs to change too, so Japanese should believe that we can do it.

## Public Transportation Systems

ERIC BARRERA

WHEN I CAME TO THE United States of America from Mexico, I didn't speak English, but I needed to work because I did not have money to survive. On my second day in this beautiful country, I was looking for job ideas, and even though I had a car, I chose to use public transportation. It was confusing. The price, the route, and the schedule were all very confusing.

I vividly remember when I rode the bus for the first time in America. I did not know how much to pay, but I remembered the price at home, and I put two dollars into the money safety box. The driver's face got red, and he yelled at me. I didn't know why. All the passengers were watching me as I contemplated my mistake. I had no idea what I had done wrong. Today I know that the regular bus and the express bus have the same route, but the price is higher for the express bus because it makes fewer stops, making the trip faster. But at that time, I didn't know the system. I wanted to cry from embarrassment. I had no language to inquire about the mistake, so the driver continued to yell at me. I froze for a couple of minutes, but it felt like two hours. I couldn't do anything because all of the passengers spoke only English.

Since then I have learned a lot about public transportation here. I know that the bus fare is different when you ride an express bus and that all the routes have two scheduled times, one for weekdays and one weekends. Some routes are from Monday to Friday and have limited hours of service. Some routes offer the service only in the morning. Other routes have service at night, but the route number changes after twelve noon. When I didn't understand English, all this information was confusing for me.

When I finally got off the bus, I walked for three hours. It was raining, and I was wearing shorts and a T-shirt. When I returned home, I described my experience to my family. They told me to learn English. Thank you, Las Positas College.

## Two Different Countries

MARIO MORA

THE UNITED STATES AND MEXICO, my native country, are very different, especially the language, the culture, the laws, and some people's beliefs. When I first arrived here, it was difficult for me to adjust to these differences.

English and Spanish have some similarities, especially the vocabulary, so I expected to understand at least something when I arrived. However, when I came to the United States nine years ago, I discovered that the two languages have completely different sounds, especially the vowels, and it was very difficult to understand, especially because I had never studied English before. I did not understand any words when people talked to me. At first, all of the words sounded like a buzzing noise. Learning English has been my goal since I came here, and I have a battle with the language every day. I study English daily, but when I am studying, I often think of being at war with the language, and I have to win. This probably doesn't help me learn, but the thoughts remain.

In spite of the language differences, I appreciate many things about American culture. People in the United States respect other people's beliefs, behavior, ideas, and property. On the contrary, in Mexico many people do not respect others. Some people even laugh when other people make mistakes. In the Unites States, people often help you if you make a mistake or seem to need help. American people also respect the laws. The laws in the United States are based on the Constitution and people follow the rules. In Mexico, most people break the law, and corruption is not uncommon. I like living with respect.

One difference that is difficult to accept is discrimination, which is more common in the United States than in Mexico. Here I have experienced discrimination because of race, skin color, and even language. That is the hardest part of living in America, and the most difficult to accept. For example, when I came to the USA, I tried to find a job, and I went to a company which had a help wanted sign up. The person who gave out the applications asked me, "Do you speak English?" but I said "Not too much." She responded, "I am sorry we do not need help now." Discrimination can break people's feelings.

There are many good things in America, but also many things that are hard to accept. Mexico and the United States are very different in many ways, but both are very nice countries.

## The Difficult and the Best

DANISH HABIB

THE UNITED STATES OF AMERICA is a great country to live in and offers inviting  opportunities for immigrants, but in addition to the best things, it has some challenges for immigrants as well. I have had difficulties with understanding the language, with adapting to the culture, and with learning a different school system.

When I first came to America, I couldn't speak English at all, and I had a hard time learning the language. For example, one day my friend took me to the store and a woman was looking for something or someone. I don't remember which. She asked me something in English, and I said, "What?" in my own language, Dari. The woman realized that I did not speak English, but not immediately. When I went home, I was sad and felt like crying because I realized that my life would never be the same. I discussed this with my father, and he gave me some good advice. He said, "Learn one new word each day. That will be thirty words each month." I took his advice, and now I still learn one new word every day.

I also had difficulty with the unfamiliar culture because the culture where I come from, Afghanistan, is totally different from the United States. For example, boys and girls go to the same school, at the same time here. In Afghanistan, however, girls go to one school, and boys go to another. All students have to wear a uniform to school there, but here that is not usually the case.

Education has been very difficult in Afghanistan for many years because of the wars. The Russian army invaded Afghanistan many years ago, and after they left, the government was not stable. Then the United States invaded the country in 2001. Consequently, I never attended school in Afghanistan. My first day of school was here in the United States at James Logan High School. I didn't know anyone there. On that first day, I was very confused. The day before school started, our family friend went to the school to get my schedule, but she forgot to explain that the numbers next to each class were room numbers. I missed the first two periods of class because I could not ask someone to show me where my classes were. Finally, a girl from Afghanistan saw me and asked me what I was looking for. She took me to my classes and helped me until I learned enough English to make my way around. She is still my best friend, and I love her a lot.

The thing that I like best about America is the educational system because anyone of any age can go to school. That is not true everywhere. In Afghanistan, for example, when people get older, they don't want to go to school. I suppose they feel ashamed because others will say that they were lazy when they were young. But here, I see people of all ages in my classes, not only ESL classes. This would not happen in Afghanistan because adults would feel ashamed to be in class with young people. Another thing I like about the educational system here is that people can come to America with no education, but they can still study here. For example, I started going to school in this country, and I am going to finish it here. In

Afghanistan, it is very difficult for girls to get an education, but now I plan to study business, and in the future, I plan to be a business woman.

Best of all, I like the equal rights in the United States because all religions are equal. For example, I am Muslim and wear a headscarf, but I can still get a job and do things other women do. Also, Muslims have been building mosques in many cities. In Afghanistan, no one could build a church or a temple. Only mosques are allowed.

When I first arrived in the USA, I only understood the difficulties. This is probably true for many people. After overcoming those difficulties, immigrants can have the best life ever.

## Coping with Differences

SABILA ASIF

WHEN I CAME TO THE United States with my family, I did not know anything about America. I had also never been on an airplane. My life experience was so different from everything here that I had to cope with many difficulties.

The most immediate difficulty was language. I realized that I couldn't live here without learning English. How could I talk with my children's teachers and doctors? In the beginning my husband had to go everywhere with me, even to the salon to have my hair cut. I also could not help my children with their homework. I will never forget the day my son came home from school and cried, telling me he did not understand what the teacher was saying. He was very upset because of the homework he was assigned. I tried to calm him down as tears ran down my face, too. I felt embarrassed and sad that I could not help my son with anything. To alleviate my difficulty, I began taking classes and learning English.

Driving was another difficulty. In Pakistan, I was a housewife. I had never gone outside of my home by myself. That is the custom there. However, in America, people have to do everything by themselves. For this reason, I had to learn to drive. In addition to shopping and other errands, I needed to drop off and pick up my children. Soon, I discovered that I could also go anywhere I wished. Getting a license was not easy. I had to pass the written test first, and I did not speak or understand English. I took the test four times before I finally passed and got my permit.

Finally, it was especially difficult to get our green cards. In the beginning, my husband worked as an engineer in a technology company. He had to work very hard because at that time technology companies were not doing well. After a few months at work, my husband was laid off. In order to keep the green card application in progress, my husband had to find another job quickly. Luckily, within a few months he found employment and our green card process continued. This process is still on-going, and we continue to hope to get our green cards in the future. The stress of wondering and waiting adds to the difficulty.

With coming to the United States, I had to leave my old life and enter a life that was difficult at first. Even though I felt as if I had been born all over again, I knew that this country had many opportunities to offer our family if we had the motivation to improve our standard of living and achieve a better education. The differences between my native country and the United States are vast and caused some difficulties at first, but as our time in America passes, those differences seem less important and the memory of the difficulties has dimmed.

## Two Little Differences

LEO LOZANO

THERE ARE TWO LITTLE DIFFERENCES between Hidalgo, a state in Mexico where I come from, and California, where I live now: driving rules and food.

In Hidalgo, we have laws similar to those in California. Many driving laws are very similar, except that in Hidalgo, no one respects the laws. When you see a stop sign in California, you must make a complete stop. In Hidalgo, people see the sign, but they continue driving.

It is easier to accept the laws here now. When I arrived here, however, I did not know most of the rules. I didn't know that a helmet is required even for bicycle riding. I didn't know that there is a button to push to make it possible to cross a street at a signal, and that pedestrians must wait for their turn. In Hidalgo, people cross the street wherever and whenever they want to, even on busy highways. There are pedestrian bridges across many busy streets and highways, but I have only seen dogs using them.

There are some other differences in the laws. In the smaller towns of Hidalgo, insurance is not mandatory, but here everyone must have automobile insurance. In California, drivers must respect pedestrians and people on bicycles, which is not the case there. I feel confident driving in California because I know and respect the rules, and I know that all the other drivers do as well. I also feel safer when I am walking.

Getting accustomed to the food in California was not as easy as learning the driving rules. In Mexico, there is a great variety in traditional dishes such as *barbacoa*, *pozole*, *menudo*, and *carnitas*. All these are very different from the local food of California. Even in Mexican restaurants, the flavor is very different because the ingredients are not the same. I wanted to cook my own food, but at first, I couldn't find the ingredients I needed such as *huitlacoche*, the mushrooms from corn, or *achiote*, a sweet potato. It probably didn't help that I could not speak English, so I could not ask for help. Now I can find the ingredients I need in a Mexican market. I also speak English, so I can ask for help in any grocery store.

I am often amused when I think of these two little differences between Hidalgo and California. I feel safe now because I understand and appreciate the differences between my two homes.

CHAPTER SIX

# So Glad I'm Here

Dreaming of College

The Best Decision of My Life

Here I Come, Sunny California!

Being Thankful!

A Second Chance

# So Glad I'm Here

## Dreaming of College

SARAH NIELSEN

*A*S A TEENAGER IN ARIZONA in the 1930s, my maternal grandmother had dreams of going to college. She loved school. She loved to read. She loved ideas. Her father, however, had different dreams for her. In his mind, girls didn't need to go to college. After graduating from high school, he expected my grandmother to work for a year or two, then get married and have children. Lula was a good girl, obedient and hardworking. She did what her father expected, but she never let go of her dream of going to college.

After working as a live-in maid for a doctor's family for a few years, she met my grandfather, and before long, they got married and had their first child. Her husband, my grandfather, was also a traditional man. He didn't want his Lula to work or go to school once they were married. When

World War II was over and my grandfather was discharged from the navy, he moved my grandmother and my mother to California where he planned to farm the land and study to become a veterinarian. He was full of vast hope and big dreams like so many other young men after the war.

Nothing was easy in California. My grandfather had left school before the age of thirteen to help his mother support his siblings after his father just up and left one day, never to be heard from again. My grandfather didn't understand the first thing about higher education. He quickly found out that he couldn't just show up at a university and start studying veterinary medicine. He didn't have much luck with farming either. Although his family never went hungry, there were many times when the electric company turned off the electricity because the bill hadn't been paid. There were many rainy nights when the water poured through the leaking roof. There were many school days for my mother and my aunt when they showed up with their toes sticking out of their old, broken shoes.

My grandmother had held her dream of going to college secretly inside herself through the family's difficult times in California. When Grant Technical College, one of the early public community colleges in the Sacramento valley, opened in the neighboring town, she knew what she had to do. For the first time in her life, she defied the men in her life. She had to. She had her girls to think of. She wanted a better life for them. She wanted a world where they could go to college and realize the dreams they had for themselves. At age 37, Lula made arrangements to ride the high school bus to Grant Technical College and began studying to become a school teacher.

After my grandmother finished her community college studies, she transferred to the local state university, where she earned a bachelor's degree, a teaching credential, and a master's degree in three years. My mother has told me that my grandmother didn't sleep much in those years. She studied late into the night while her husband and her daughters slept. After receiving her undergraduate and graduate degrees, my grandmother worked for many years as an elementary school teacher and improved her family's financial situation a great deal. My mother and my aunt, Lula's daughters, went to college and followed the dreams they made for themselves, just like my grandmother had wanted.

At the time my grandmother went to college, it was very unusual for a middle-aged women to do this. Now, there are many people in the USA who go to college for various reasons and at various times in their lives. In fact, I think the community college system in America is one of the most democratic higher education systems in the world. It is one aspect of the United States that makes me proud. It has helped my family and countless others realize their dreams.

## The Best Decision of My Life

BRENDA PINEDA

MOVING TO THE UNITED STATES was the best change in my life because this country has provided many of the biggest experiences in my life, and I have learned much from these experiences. There are three reasons I am grateful for living in this country: the language, the culture, and the security.

The first reason is the language. Learning to use a language in addition to your native language is very difficult, but it is also very interesting and rewarding. For example, when I started to learn English, I was very scared because some people made fun of my bad English. Now I don't care because I speak the language better than they do. I remember one day when my friend Guadalupe accompanied me to see the doctor. The doctor asked me, "Do you have a headache?" I answered, "Yes, and I had tomorrow." My friend laughed at my mistake, made fun of me, and told our other friends all about it. Now, Guadalupe asks me to translate for her when she goes to the doctor.

The second reason is the culture, which is very fun because there is a lot to learn about how American traditions are celebrated. For example, there is Thanksgiving, the day of turkey and gratitude. I love this day because I can spend time giving thanks for everything I have received during the year. Last Thanksgiving I shared this tradition with my daughter. We cooked turkey using a Mexican-style recipe, and she has decided to celebrate this holiday for the rest of her life.

The last and most important reason is the security of this country. Compared to Mexico, the streets of the United States are very safe. I feel my family and I live a secure life in this country. For example, here it is not common for a house to be robbed, but in Mexico it happens every day. In fact, I personally know many people who have been robbery victims. The murder rate here is also lower than it is in Mexico.

For all of these reasons, I love living in the USA, and to this day, I am sure that moving to this country was the best decision of my life. My daughter, my husband, and I have learned a new language, and we enjoy the holidays of this country and appreciate the secure life we have here.

# Here I Come, Sunny California!

## LENKA ADAMOVA

COMING TO THE UNITED STATES has been my dream since I was sixteen or so. I left my home country, the Czech Republic, right after graduating from high school and moved to London for two years, where I was working as an au pair. After that, I decided to come to the USA for one year. I was not worried or anxious about living abroad since I was used to that. I was mostly excited about starting a new experience. I was used to working as an au pair, so I knew what to expect and what was expected of me. To my surprise, everything turned out to be different from what I had imagined!

After my arrival, I was welcomed by my host family at the airport. I was very glad that they looked like very nice, down-to-earth people. But I was also realistic and understood that I was here to work for them first and then make friends. The first few weeks went by, and things were going well. Additionally, I became very good friends with my host mom and enjoyed looking after her little girl, who was only four years old at that time. I was very happy that everything was going so smoothly. I found quite a few friends, most of them nannies or moms. We would meet with "our" kids every day and spend most of our days together. It was so much fun for all of us.

When it came to my English, my biggest problem was using British words like trousers, nappies, jumper, and supper. My host family would always laugh along with me. From my early days in the United States, I started noticing major differences between British and American English. I was also taking English classes at the adult school, though interestingly, I found those not as useful as just hanging out with native speakers. That was the key to learning everyday American English. And that's just what I wanted.

When it came to adapting my lifestyle to the "American way" of living, I had no problem at all. My most pleasant surprise was finding out that here in America people don't iron their clothes. I was used to hours of ironing every single week, and here my host family didn't even know where their iron was! And, of course, who would have trouble adapting to beautiful California weather? I was used to rain pretty much all year round in London, so living here felt like paradise to me. I just kept driving everywhere, exploring new places. I have always loved the coast the most. It was just so magical to me the first time I saw it, and it still is to this day. I used to drive to Santa Cruz to have lunch at the beach or just while away a nice Sunday afternoon. My first summer here, my friends and I went to San Diego for a vacation. It was the best vacation of my life, and I fell in love with Mission Beach, Pacific Beach, and of course, La Jolla Beach. Another beautiful place I visited my first year here was Santa Barbara. My host mom's brother lived there at that time, so we went to see him and his family. I had my friend with me, so during the day, we just hung out downtown, browsing through interesting galleries and shops. At night, we checked out a few clubs.

I have to admit that my biggest surprise about living in the USA was how friendly people were to me. I was used to being looked down upon in England because of the fact that I'm from eastern Europe. But that wasn't the case with the people I worked for and met in the United States. Very soon I found quite a few extra babysitting jobs and got to know many families. I have always thought that being surrounded by good, positive people is important, and there were a few friends here whom I had to stop talking to because they just kept gossiping on and on. By choosing to end these friendships, I managed to avoid a lot of the unnecessary drama they were causing and spent more time with those friends who had a positive outlook.

It has been exactly seven years since I came to live in the USA. Looking back now, I wouldn't change a thing. I got married, and I'm working to complete my degree in nursing. What I've learned is that if you give the best of yourself to others, the best will come back to you in one way or another. All I can say is that I'm grateful for all the blessings and special people I have in my life.


## Being Thankful!
JAMILA FAROOQI

$\mathcal{W}$HEN I WAS IN MY country, Afghanistan, there was so much war there that my husband and I decided to go to Pakistan. We got our plane tickets and flew to Pakistan with our children. We lived there for seven years, waiting until our paperwork to come to the USA was done. Finally, we arrived in the USA, and I was so happy to come here. All my family—my mother, my father, my three sisters, and five brothers—live here. They met me at the San Francisco airport after ten long years of separation. My family and I were all so happy to see each other. My husband and my children were also very excited to see my family after such a long time, but none of us was sure about the lifestyle here.

When I came to the United States, I didn't know English very well. I didn't know how to drive, and once I started to learn, I found it difficult, too. But I went to adult school for many years to learn English, and later on, I joined the ESL program at Las Positas College. Now I know English, and I have a job I like, too. I even learned to drive and I have my driver license.

At first, it was difficult to accept that people here live differently than in my country. When I came to the USA, in the first two or three years, the differences were especially noticeable and difficult because I am a Muslim woman. I was unsure whether my children and I would have a happy life here or whether we could study and find jobs. All these questions were in my mind, but very soon and very easily I came to realize that this country is the best country with open-minded people where all are free to practice their religion. I also like living here because everyone can study, live wherever they want, and seek a job that interests them. No one tells us that we cannot work or live or study somewhere. No one tells us what kind of clothes to wear or what kind of religion to practice. Now I am a teacher's assistant in a preschool. My children, who grew up here, have studied and found meaningful work as well. They have become more religious because they have learned about their religion and taught it to young Muslim children living here.

The main difference is that there was war in my country, but there is no war here. Another difference is that in my country women could not go to the mosque, but here we are happy that we can go to the mosque and meet other people of our faith. Despite these differences, there are a lot of similarities between my life in Afghanistan and my life in America. For example, I went to college in my country, and here I'm going to college as well. I was a teacher in a middle school in my country, and here I am a teacher's assistant. In my country, I owned a house, and here I am renting a house. Here in every city, we have the same Afghani shops that we had in my country. In these shops, we can find everything we need from fresh Afghani bread and fresh meat to basmati rice and Afghani cookies. There are also restaurants here that prepare the same dishes as restaurants in Afghanistan and clothing shops that sell the same fashions as shops in Afghanistan.

## A Second Chance

GIANNA FERNANDEZ

ᴌIVING IN THE USA IS the result of big changes in my life, changes that have made me into the person that I am today. Everything started when my life broke apart. One day, when I was feeling as happy and complete as a person can feel, everything changed. After eight years of friendship, I married my best friend. "What can be better than this?" I thought. We knew each other very well, so what could go wrong? I really thought that to make a marriage work you wouldn't need many things but a good friendship. In time, it became obvious that wasn't enough. After three years of marriage, I was expecting a child. Three months later we broke up. As a result, I would confront the most difficult times of my life. I was pregnant with the baby I always dreamed of having. I had been working in my own business, and I was finishing decorating the new house that we would move into soon. There was only one thing missing: My best friend "husband" didn't want to be part of our life anymore.

I had to figure out how to pull myself together and continue without him. After that, it took me several months to decide what to do. Meanwhile, one of my brothers sent me an open ticket to San Francisco so that I would be able to take some time to consider the situation. I flew to San Francisco, where my brothers were waiting for me, and there I spent the next five months of my pregnancy.

During this stage of my pregnancy, I felt very blessed to have my brothers with me. It was definitely a whole new experience for the three of us. For example, I remember that my oldest brother would take me to nice places like restaurants, theaters and even parties with his friends. The only bad thing was that he had to stop very often for me to breathe some fresh air because I was feeling pretty sick. Besides that, he used to go with me to the doctor every month and take care of my necessities. It was very impressive. He did everything for me, from taking the time off from work to putting off his other activities as a single man. It must have been hard on him, but he did it for me anyway. And that is something that I will always remember.

Just like my older brother, the youngest one was helping me satisfy my cravings as a pregnant woman. For example, one night I was feeling pretty sad, and I cried for many hours. Suddenly and crazily, I wanted lemon pie from the Cheese Cake Factory, which at that time was only in San Francisco. I didn't wait one minute. I called him hoping that he would bring that delicious pie to me. There was just one little inconvenience with this plan, which was that I was living in Fremont and he was living in San Francisco. He was working while I was at home. The probability of getting that pie the same night was small. At this point, realizing I might not get my pie, I was feeling pretty anxious.

Later that night, my brother showed up on my doorstep with a big bag from the Cheese Cake Factory. He had tied a big butterfly helium balloon to the bag handles. Inside the bag, there was, obviously, a big piece of my favorite lemon pie, which I can almost taste again right now. This is another special moment I will keep in my mind forever. It is not only because of the delicious pie, but also because of the kindness and consideration my brother showed me.

After four months, I felt better and stronger; I went back to Ecuador to deliver my baby. When I arrived, I moved to the new house. And by living there I was hoping to find a second opportunity for my marriage with the company and support of my parents and friends. During that time, I was also trying to keep myself busy by seeing things from a different perspective. It was so clear that my husband and I both had been trying to make everybody happy around us, but we weren't succeeding. So, I started to consider the possibility of regaining some independence, and most of all, some peace. Therefore, I agreed with my son's father that I would give up our house, car, and material things in exchange for the freedom to raise my son in the way I believed would be appropriate for him.

This agreement was shocking at first, but at that point, it was the only option. Consequently, the last hope I had vanished in front of my eyes. That day, as a result of his coldness towards the situation, I made the decision to move to California in six months. For all these reasons, I am now living in the USA. All in all, these big changes in my life gave me the opportunity to learn many things about myself and about second chances in life. I learned that material possessions cannot give you happiness.

CHAPTER SEVEN

# The Good
# and the Bad

Both/And

The Strong and the Weak

Closings and Openings

The Foreign Student Life

English is Key

# The Good
# and the Bad

## Both/And

SARAH NIELSEN

*A*T LAS POSITAS COLLEGE, ESL students usually read about African American history in the spring semester. Sometimes when I mention that fact to friends or relatives, they frown and look concerned. They ask me if it's really a good idea for people who are studying in the United States or who have immigrated here to read about slavery or Jim Crow laws since these are some of the ugliest and most shameful parts of this nation's history. "Shouldn't ESL students read about the good and noble parts of American history?" they ask.

On one hand, I certainly agree that slavery, segregation, and other injustices that African Americans have suffered are ugly and shameful. It can be very painful to learn more about this part of American history and to discover that racism still exists here. On the other hand, I think about the ways in which people of African origins have made the United States a better nation by forcing the government to live up to its ideals of freedom and democracy. I feel proud to be an American when I think about an activist like Rosa Parks, an African American whose actions helped to end the Jim Crow practice of buses segregated into white and black sections. I feel proud to be an American when I think about how the the National Association for the Advancement of Colored People (NAACP) used the federal court system to end the legal segregation of schools here.

Unfortunately, there are many other groups of people who have suffered and still suffer because of prejudice in the United States. But these groups have also pushed this country to more closely follow the noble principles that the nation was built on. For example, the Fair Play Boys and others of Japanese origins used the federal court system to prove that Japanese internment during World War II was unconstitutional. It was because of their fight that the internment camps were closed and that Japanese Americans eventually received an apology and reparations from the government.

As a white American, I feel strongly that Rosa Parks and the Fair Play Boys are also part of my history and part of the history of the larger United States. Although I am not proud of Jim Crow laws, Japanese internment, and countless other injustices, I am proud that this is a country where people of every background can and do fight to transform this nation into a more just place.

# The Strong and the Weak

JIN RYOO

*H*AVING THE OPPORTUNITY TO LIVE in the USA was a stroke of good luck for me. After having spent several years here, I realize that there are some good and bad points about living here.

One strong point is the nice weather, especially here in California where it seems perfect all the time. In my country, Korea, it is too hot and humid in the summer season, and too cold and icy in the winter season. I do love experiencing four distinct seasons, but in California, every day has perfect weather for outdoor activities. It is warm enough in the winter, and the summer air isn't too humid. Like I said, perfect!

Another strong point is that the USA is heaven for consumers. Everywhere I go shopping, there's a huge and convenient parking lot. But the refund policy was a kind of culture shock for me. A customer who is not satisfied with a product or who simply has changed her mind about a product can get a refund. This is a great system for consumers, though some people abuse it. I think this could result in higher prices for products, which consumers will end up paying for in the end.

One weak point is a lack of participation in the recycling system to preserve the environment. In my country, people have to sort their trash. If they don't, they will have to pay a fine. In the USA, people don't seem to care much about trash and recycling. Whenever I use disposable cups or plates for my convenience, I feel guilty. I try to avoid using disposables as much as possible, choosing paper over plastic products to help the environment when I do have to use disposables.

Another weak point in the USA is the high cost of health insurance. I can have very high quality medical care in the USA, but I have to buy very expensive health insurance to get that good care. People who can't afford good insurance don't have access to good health care. In fact, many people don't have any medical insurance and can't see a doctor for their health needs because they simply can't afford the cost. I think the government should consider a different system, one that addresses the problem of unequal treatment of human beings.

In my opinion, the United States has good conditions for people who have enough money, but it needs to consider the environment and medical care more for the good of all people.

## Closings and Openings
### ANONYMOUS

COMING TO THE USA WAS the most important decision that I have ever made. My family and I received political asylum because we suffered persecution from a terrorist group because of our ideas. When I arrived here in 2004, I remember being in shock because everything was different from my country. I had to leave everything behind there: my customs, my relatives, my friends, and my job. Suddenly in a very short period of time, my life changed completely. I had to learn about the American culture, language, and law. Everything was new to me and my family.

The first difficulty was the language. We needed to learn to speak, read, and write in English. We found an adult school in Pleasanton with an ESL program and started to study there about two hours every day. I remember something funny that happened early in our ESL studies. The teacher asked my wife and me a simple question, and neither of us understood anything at all!

The second difficulty was how people felt about immigrants. I had to fight against the stereotype that immigrants are ignorant people. The people who think that are WRONG! From my experience, most immigration in California is from Central and South America. A high percentage of Latino immigrants work here, but don't study. This means they have to work in jobs that don't require education. Most of these workers don't speak English or even know their rights as human beings. I have had to suffer discrimination many times because of my English skills. I remember applying for a job in a store and getting an interview. The person conducting the interview asked many questions, some of which were very difficult to answer. I felt very sad when the interviewer smiled and said, "Come back when you understand English." This experience pushed me to study English here at Las Positas College.

Despite these difficulties, I am very happy to be living in the United States because this country has given me peace and many valuable experiences. I have had the chance to make new friends and keep my family together. I want to say sincerely: God bless America forever.

# The Foreign Student Life

DEWI PETRINASIH PUTRI

LIFE IS NOT EASY. I have heard this expression so many times, but never did I think I would be the one using it. I had always been comfortable living with my parents, and I never had to worry about money for food or for education. My parents did all the worrying for me. After all, I was a teenager then. Living with my parents was fun and stress free, and I wish those moments could have lasted forever. About a year ago, I decided to leave my native country and come to the United States to continue my studies. When I got here, I suddenly turned into someone labeled "foreign student." A foreign student, I discovered, has more problems to face than the average American students do. Whether from Indonesia, like me, or from some other country, a foreign student has to work twice as hard as Americans do in order to succeed academically. Living in America as a foreign student means facing a lot of challenges and responsibilities.

The language barrier is one of the problems faced by foreign students. American students have the advantage of comprehending English without working too hard; however, some of them still complain that some professors talk too fast, mumble, or use big words. As a result, they cannot take notes fast enough to keep up, or they misunderstand what the instructor says. For foreign students, the burden of understanding the lectures is twice as hard because English is their second language. Because of this, they have limited comprehension and understanding. Moreover, many Americans use slang, which is hard to understand. Words and phrases such as "What's up?", "messed up," or "hassle" make it difficult for foreign students to understand and socialize with other students. The language barrier makes the life of a foreign student in America harder because it doubles the load of challenges that they have to face such as learning a second language and maintaining good academic standing.

In addition to the language barrier, another problem I am facing is adjusting to the American classroom. I really am a stranger here, and many things are different from what I have known before. For instance, the academic system in America is very different from the one in Indonesia. In the United States, instructors seem to treat students with respect equal to a peer. Many classes are informal, and the relationship between the instructor and students is cordial. In fact, students call some instructors by their first names. In Indonesia, however, the relationship between instructors and students is more formal. Lectures are conducted in a very formal way. Students show their respect by listening quietly and paying attention at all times. The casual American atmosphere makes me feel uncomfortable in class because I am used to the Indonesian classroom setting.

Perhaps the most difficult problem I face is living in a different community. American students may have some trouble making new friends or may feel lonely at times. However, they usually manage to find other people with the same background, interests, and goals. For a foreign student like me, it is twice as hard to make new friends, although making small talk with other students can lead to a friendship. I find it difficult to become friends with other students because I do not understand some aspects of the American way of living. The American and Indonesian cultures have huge differences, and many students would rather talk to someone who has a similar cultural background to their own. Not having friends, with whom I could share good and bad moments, makes it harder for me not to feel lonely and homesick.

Despite all the hardships that I have faced and must overcome as a foreign student, I would not give up the chance to study here in the United States. Each day, the problems seem a little bit less overwhelming. Like a little child who is finally learning to read, write, and make sense of things around me, I have started to enjoy my experience of discovering a brand new world.

## English is Key

HUGO VERA

LIVING IN THE USA HAS been full of experiences. Some experiences have been good and some difficult, but the overall experience has been extraordinary. The most difficult part of living in the United States has been to learn English. When I first came here, fortunately, I found a job as a dishwasher in a Chinese restaurant. I ended up working there because I could not speak English. At that time, I noticed that learning English was necessary, but I didn't pay too much attention to it. I thought, "I have Latino friends that speak English, and I can ask them for help translating the language." How wrong I was! The next week, when I got some money, I went to the store to get some food. When I was ready to pay, the cashier started to talk to me, but I didn't understand anything. I didn't know what she was saying. I felt ashamed. I just gave her a hundred dollar bill. She returned my change, and I left. Then I really thought: It is time to learn English.

I knew some words from the education I had in Mexico such as *door, window, chair, hello, my name is,* but these were only simple and easy words I had memorized. I didn't know how to formulate a sentence. I didn't even know how to pronounce words. Around the time I became more aware of my English needs, I found another job in a construction company, where the majority of the workers were Americans, and I learned English just a little bit better. I bought some English books including a Spanish-English dictionary, and I started to read and repeat what I read. I went to the stores and tried to talk with shoppers and store clerks, but they didn't understand me very well. I felt frustrated. I decided to go to English school, so I attended Almond Adult School. That didn't work well for me, either. In adult schools, people can join the English courses at any time. There is no homework or program to follow. Now I have been living here for seven years. Since I started studying ESL at Las Positas College, I am really learning to read, write, and speak English. It is hard, of course, but I am putting my best foot forward.

How has living in the United States changed my life? Well, since I can communicate with people here in America, I notice that here there are opportunities to be successful or to achieve your personal goals. You can work and study. This is something that is difficult to do in my country. Once you speak English, the doors open themselves. Here in the USA you can do what you most like to do, and I believe that this is the best part. Now I am in an intermediate ESL class. As soon as I finish all the ESL levels, I will try to enroll at the university in Hayward and eventually get a Teachers of English to Speakers of Other Languages (TESOL) certificate to teach English in my country.

The changes in my life have also meant changes in my family's life. Now I am the crew leader for a group of roofers in the company where I work. I am providing all the necessary things for my family such as food, health care, our own house, and a good education. My life in the United States has not been easy, but thanks to the opportunities, to my decision to come live here, and especially to this great nation itself, my life has been very full and happy.

CHAPTER EIGHT

# Amusing Memories

Street Signs

A Bud on the Patio?

Te Quiero

Lotion Works Best

Memories of Trouble

# Amusing Memories

## Street Signs

MARILYN MARQUIS

*I*N 1987, I TOOK AN excursion to Japan. My mother had visited Japan several years before and had never stopped talking about how much she enjoyed that trip. My former exchange student was living in Hokkaido, the northern most island in Japan, and I wanted to meet her husband and daughter. I had also been studying Japanese and learning about Japanese culture. So I had many reasons for wanting to visit Japan.

By then, I had been teaching ESL for several years and many of my students were from Japan, so I had a ready source of suggestions when I asked them what I should see on my trip. They suggested cities, restaurants, stores, parks, and museums. I scheduled my trip for spring break because I longed to see the famous cherry blossoms in bloom. The rest of my itinerary came from students.

I was a little nervous about going to a country where the writing system was very different from my own, but I felt confident then because I had so much help with preparations. I also had some friends in Japan who were eager to be my guides at least some of the time. The first week, I had a tour guide for at least part of every day and enjoyed going to museums and temples, eating delicious Japanese food, and window shopping in Ginza, a world famous shopping area.

My trip to Hokkaido was also easier than I anticipated. I memorized the *kanji* for each sign at the airport and at the train station. I knew what city names to look for so that I would get off in the right place. My Japanese daughter, Yoko, was waiting for me with her family, and we had several days together. Unlike Tokyo, where tourists from all over the world were a common sight, in Hokkaido, I was a star, or at least an oddity. We went to a grocery store, just like I had taken her many years before, and little children came up to touch me, or to just look. When we went to a restaurant, a little boy came to our table with his camera to take my picture. Perhaps he wanted to prove to his friends that he had really seen a foreigner. All was very pleasing.

When I returned to Tokyo, I would be on my own for the final few days of my trip. I did very well getting from the airport to the train and getting on the correct train for my destination. I had the hotel name and the street address all memorized in *kanji*. I had selected a hotel that was walking distance from the train station, so all I needed was to find the street just outside the train station. This is where the problems began. I walked out of the train station and looked for a street sign at the first corner I came to. There was no sign, but I didn't worry. I walked back into the train station and went out a different exit, still looking for a street sign. No sign. I returned to the train station and tried the same thing at the other two exits. I felt rather frustrated, but I fancied myself a very clever person and decided to just get in a cab and tell the driver where I wanted to go. I gave the driver the name of the hotel and the name of the street and he looked at me in a way that indicated that he thought I was, well, strange. He pulled around the corner and said, "This is it," I got out and felt rather foolish. I checked into the hotel and decided to do a little investigating. I went for a walk and looked for street signs at every corner. Not one street sign did I find. Not one. For the next few days, I looked for street signs throughout the city. There are none. Tokyo is one of the largest cities in the world and exists without street signs. I wondered how taxi drivers, or any drivers, or walkers could manage to find their way around.

I returned home and asked my students about the street signs and why no one had thought to tell me in advance that I might have some trouble because of that. I learned that many of my businessmen students and their wives had never driven in Japan. They simply had not noticed that there were no street signs.

## A Bud on the Patio?

SARAH JEONG

WHEN I CAME TO THE USA, everything was difficult. I was immediately confronted by differences in language, food, and etiquette. A lot of funny things resulted from my limitations with the English language, but two are particularly amusing to me.

Once, when my family was living in a small apartment, after my husband went to his office, my kids and I discovered a dead bird on the patio. We were quite surprised and wondered what to do. We decided to go to the apartment office to report the bird to the apartment manager. I tried to explain that there was a dead bird on the patio, but the manager didn't understand me. She thought I said, "Bud" and wondered why I would tell her about beer on the patio. She gestured the act of drinking to confirm her understanding of what I had said, so I decided to use a gesture to demonstrate my actual meaning. First, I drew a line across my neck with my hand, and then flapped my arms as if they were wings. Finally, she understood me and we both laughed. Then she sent someone to retrieve the dead bird.

My language skills are much better now, but I continue to find myself in confusing, but amusing situations because I didn't understand what someone said. A few months ago, the mother of my daughter's friend said, "Let's hang out sometime." I replied, "OK," but actually I didn't understand what she really meant. I came home and thought about things I could hang outside. Later, I decided to search for the expression on a slang list from the Internet. There I discovered that "hang out" is very different from "hang out together." I realized that she wanted to spend time together.

Now I enjoy living in the USA and find these misunderstandings quite amusing.

# Te Quiero

*M*OST IMMIGRANTS HAVE INTERESTING EXPERIENCES when they first arrive in the United States and do not have strong English language skills. Many of these early experiences were embarrassing to me when they happened, but some of my early encounters with people are a source of great amusement for me now.

For example, when I first came to the United States, I arrived in New Mexico and stayed there for a few days and then continued on to California in a travel trailer. We stopped at a gasoline station along the way, and I wanted to go to the restroom. I went into the store at the gas station and saw a tall black man who looked like a businessman. He wore a suit and looked very decent. I thought he would be willing to help me. I asked him where the restroom was in Spanish, but he didn't understand me. I decided to use gestures to show what I meant, so I pretended to take off my jeans. The man was very surprised and started saying, "No. No. Wait! Whoa!" He clearly thought I was gesturing to express a very different idea. I was very embarrassed.

After I got settled in an apartment, I developed a friendship with my neighbors. One neighbor, a nice American guy, invited me to go to Carl's Jr. with him. When we got to Carl's Jr., he asked me what size hamburger I wanted. My friends had told me that most people in California speak some Spanish and since I didn't really speak English, I answered in Spanish. I said, *"chica"* which means small. However, he thought that I said I wanted a chicken burger. It was immediately clear that he didn't understand Spanish.

Later, I developed a friendship with a man from India. We worked together and had similar hours, so he often

120 ∾ LIVING IN THE USA

offered to drive me home after work. He could speak a little bit of Spanish, so I thought he was speaking Spanish when he dropped me off. When we arrived at my place, I always said, "Thank you. Goodbye." He always said, "*Te quiero.*" At least that is what I thought he said. It did seem strange that he would say, "I love you." But I didn't want to act surprised or shocked. Eventually, I realized that he actually said, "Take care." I still laugh when I think of my mistake.

When I remember how I could not say a single word in English and how I often misunderstood what I heard, I recognize my progress in just a few years. These amusing events were perhaps not so funny to me at the time, but they are very amusing now. I am glad that I can find humor when I remember how hard it was to learn English. It motivates me to continue studying.

## Lotion Works Best
### ANONYMOUS

MY GREATEST DIFFICULTY WHEN I arrived in this country was with the language. Before I came here, I felt confident about using English because I had studied English in my country. Immediately after I arrived in the United States, I realized that my assumption was totally wrong. I didn't understand anything. At first, I thought it was the pronunciation because everyone spoke very fast and nothing was clear. That also proved not to be the case. The real issues were my limited vocabulary and my lack of understanding the culture.

I initially dealt with the language problem by asking for help from Latin people who could speak English. It became my routine to request help from others for everything in my daily life. This solution worked very well for me as long as a friend was available. One day, however, I went to the store by myself. I needed lotion and thought I certainly could buy lotion without help. I bought a bottle of Nivea and went home. Later, after I took a shower, I put the Nivea on my skin. Within a very short time, my skin was dry, so I applied more lotion. Then I felt itchy, and my skin was irritated. A friend later asked me about my skin problem, so I explained that I had purchased lotion, but it didn't seem to help my dry skin. She asked to see the lotion. She looked at the bottle and looked at me, then began to laugh. I had purchased shampoo and was putting it directly on my skin and rubbing it in as if it were lotion.

My friend and I laughed at the time, but I felt very bad that I could not go to the store for necessities and feel confident. I decided then that I would register for ESL classes at Las Positas College and work toward mastering English. If I had not made that decision, who knows what I might have put on my skin next!

## Memories of Troubles

GRACE

WE BOARDED THE AIRPLANE HEADING to the USA full of excitement and expectations, but our lives in the new country were not always easy. My husband was a graduate student, and we were so excited about living a student life in English.

The most difficult thing early in our stay was communicating our needs. We didn't know where the market was located, and when we found it, we had a difficult time finding what we needed because the packaging was in English. We would sometimes ask a friend or fellow student for help with things we needed, but that was not always reliable. For example, once my husband asked a classmate, also a foreign student, for information about a class. When they arrived in class the following day, they had both done the wrong homework. After that, he was more careful about whom he asked for help.

Sometimes we didn't know that we should ask questions. Once we decided to take a summer vacation to see some famous places on the East Coast as we were on our way to a conference in Chicago. We went to Niagara Falls first and were astonished by the beauty of this natural attraction. After walking along the falls and experiencing the roar of all that water cascading over the falls, we were ready to head toward Chicago. We hadn't made reservations because we wanted to be flexible. Around 6 PM, we started to look for a hotel. We stopped at a Holiday Inn and were surprised that there were no rooms available. We got back in the car and drove further expecting to find a place along the highway. After a few miles, we stopped at another hotel and were again told that there were no rooms available. This was more surprising, but we were not worried. However, after stopping at four more hotels with our two young children following their daddy into the lobby each time only to return to the car with sad faces, we began to worry. No one had told us that on the July Fourth weekend, we would not find any vacancies in hotels.

Finally, we decided to sleep in the car at a rest area. No one slept well. We were all uncomfortable. Eventually we put a blanket on the ground and slept there. We all laid down and napped very comfortably. As we lay there, we saw beautiful stars in the night sky and started to count them. We had our own fireworks display provided by nature. Our family may have looked homeless, but we had a good time.

My children remember the trip fondly. They are grown up now and have learned about American history and culture. Now they are my most effective teachers. They also help me not be embarrassed by misunderstandings.

CHAPTER NINE

# Loving People
# and Places

# Loving People and Places

## Summary Love

SARAH NIELSEN

ONE OF MY FAVORITE JOURNEYS is the one between Sacramento and Stinson Beach in the summer. On this trip, a traveler goes from the hot, dry central valley of California farm lands to the cool, lush, wild coast north of San Francisco. After we learned to drive, my high school friends and I would beg to borrow a car from one of our parents. Once a car and a Saturday were secured, we would pack our towels, bathing suits, and a big picnic lunch and head out for Stinson.

The drive took almost three hours as we made our way from the valley floor in Sacramento through almond and peach orchards to the rolling hills of Vacaville and Fairfield, golden with wild oats dried by the summer's heat and dotted with the green of hefty old oak trees. From the hills, we would turn north and then west again, driving over the northern tip of the San Francisco Bay and finally onto the mountain road that wound through damp redwood forests full of ferns and wild orchids.

About five miles before arriving at the beach, we would see it, from up on the top of Mount Tamalpais, that long stretch of sand and that seemingly endless Pacific Ocean. Even our teenage selves—usually obsessed with all things trivial, usually disdainful of pesky kids and boring adults— could not help but stop for a moment in the present, in quiet wonder of the beauty before us.

Our last trip together to Stinson Beach was just after we graduated from high school and just before we went to work or off to college. Erica, Vonnie, Georgina, Linda, Leanne, and Sarah. Sacramento valley girls who loved the ocean and who loved each other.

At one point on that last trip, we were sitting on the bluffs above the beach, and Erica started to cry.

"Erica, why are you crying?" we asked.

"It will never be like this again," she answered.

She was wiser than the rest of us. We couldn't see that truth, yet. We wrapped our arms around her as we watched the waves crash on our beloved Stinson Beach.

## The Things We Do for Love

BERTRAM RETTENMAIER

*A* SHORT VACATION TO THE USA is a great adventure. You can plan it very well, and the restrictions regarding permissions and passports are not too bad. If you want to stay longer than a vacation, it becomes more difficult and bureaucratic.

In 2007, my fiancée got an offer from her company to work for a subsidiary located in California. The agreement was to work and live there for at least three years. This was not an amount of time we wanted to live apart from each other, especially when we had just planned our wedding! The other difficulty was leaving all our family, friends, and hobbies behind. Still, we didn't want to miss the opportunity to live in a different place and experience a different culture. (Actually, the culture in the USA is not that different from that of Germany, maybe just a little bigger and more diverse, but this is a topic for another essay.) When my company moved to a new location one hour further west of our home in Germany, our decision to move to California was determined and finalized.

My fiancée signed the contract to work in the USA for three years starting in March, but with permission to travel back to Germany for our planned wedding. Another stipulation was that my fiancée's company would take care of my work permit in the USA. In order not to lose out on relocation compensation from my own company, I had to keep my job until the middle of the year.

We got our visas, which we had to apply for in person in Frankfurt, and my fiancée traveled to the USA to check out the area and find an apartment. Meanwhile, we were told that the work permit process would take up to five months. As I had wanted to start working in the USA in October, we had to be married earlier than we had planned. Not being married meant I couldn't apply for a work permit, so we moved our wedding date up and got married earlier. That's why we now have two wedding dates, an official one and a church one. (Actually, many people in Germany have two wedding dates.)

With all the documents finally in order, I was able to apply for a work permit, but I had to be in the United States to apply. I had to produce a copy of my I-94 form, which meant I had to fly to the United States to file this form in person. The good side of this requirement was having a one-week vacation, seeing my fiancée, and interviewing at the company where I would start working. Despite these positive experiences, I don't see a compelling reason— other than adding to air pollution—that I needed to fly thousands of miles to pick up a copy of my I-94 in person in the United States. I wonder to whom the bureaucrats reported the points I racked up during my flight for the world championship of air pollution!

Anyway, this story does have a happy ending. In July, we got married for a second time and had a big party with family and friends. Soon after that, I quit my old job without a glitch. And now, here we are, both of us, on planet Earth, living in California.

## Finding Love in Fremont

JUN XIA SHI

MY LIFE HAS CHANGED IN the USA. I have been here for about ten years now. I was a student when I first came to the United States. I attended a business school on a student visa. By moving to the USA, I realize I lost a big part of my life at home, and at the same time, a lot of amazing things have happened to me here. From a young lady, I became a woman. I discovered what was important in my life. I wanted to experience more.

When I first came to the USA, I could not speak English. I was alone. I could not imagine what was going to happen the next day. I stayed in Fremont on an old friend's couch for about half a year before I found my own place to live. I met some new friends who showed me a lot of interesting places. During these times, I was happy to start a new life, but the good times didn't last. I felt alone and far away from my family. I wanted to return home for a visit, but I could not because of the September 11, 2001 terrorist attacks. I was afraid if I went back to China, I could not return to the United States. I didn't know what I should do.

One important day in my life, I met a nice American guy. He was a co-worker of my friend's husband, and that is how we met. I still remember our first date was at a bar in Fremont. We enjoyed talking about our life and the future. After falling in love and dating for two years, we got married in Las Vegas. It was the most amazing day of my life.

Since that day, many other good things have come my way. I got to return to China for a visit after not seeing my family for four years. I'm married to a wonderful, loving man. We own a house, and I'm back in school, looking forward to furthering my education. My life has changed in good ways.

## Love and Loss
ANONYMOUS

*I* CAME TO THE USA TWO years ago to marry my husband, Steve. We met on the Internet, and we had kept in contact for almost a year before his first visit to see me in Thailand. After several visits, we decided to get married, and I moved to the USA. I have found that living in the USA is not easy, and it has completely changed my life forever.

There are many differences between the USA and Thailand. First of all, the weather here is colder in the winter. I have to wear a warm jacket, a sweater, gloves, and boots. In Thailand, it is hot and humid all year round, so all of my clothes before were light and summery. Another difference is food. In the USA, people eat more bread and meat, whereas in Thailand people eat more rice, fish, and vegetables. Also, people in the USA tend to cook at home because it is cheaper than going out to eat. In Thailand, street food and farmers' markets are everywhere. The food is cheap, fresh, and bountiful, and many people eat out a lot. A final difference is transportation. In the USA, everything is pretty spread out, so driving is necessary. In Thailand, there are lots of transportation options, especially in Bangkok, where there are subways, sky trains, buses, and taxis. I didn't need to drive a car in Thailand, but I had to learn to drive here.

Adjusting to differences has been hard, but it's been even harder to be far away from my family. I don't have any relatives or friends here. I am used to being around a lot of people because I grew up in the countryside with four sisters and one brother. We are all very close. Before getting married, my sisters and I lived in the city. On weekends and holidays, we would see each other or travel home together to visit our parents. Here, I can't do that anymore. I have to be satisfied with phone calls, asking from a distance what they are doing and telling them how much I miss them.

My life has really changed a lot since I came here. When I was in Thailand, I used to work as a junior engineer in a hard drive company. When I got married and moved to the USA, it was almost a year before I was eligible to work.

Once I could apply for jobs legally, it was still hard because my English wasn't good enough to land a position. This made me confused about what path I should take and why I came here in the first place. I was terribly sad and missed my family, friends, and Thailand a lot. I had been independent before, living on my own, making my own decisions. I had my own world and my own space in Thailand. But in the USA, living as a housewife, I had none of that. I had married someone totally different from me in nationality and culture. It was very hard at first, adjusting to a new country, a new environment, a new culture, and married life all at the same time. Finally, I decided to go back to school and learn English. I also decided to take a new career path and began my studies to become a nurse.

My family worried about me a lot when I first moved to the USA. Now they know that I am doing okay, so they don't worry as much as before. I know they still miss me a lot, and I still miss them, too. Even my father, who usually keeps his emotions to himself, has told me he misses me.

It hasn't been easy to live in the USA, but it has taught me to be strong, to keep learning, and to remember that adjusting to a new life in a new country takes time.

## Moving for Marriage
ANONYMOUS

MY COMING TO THE USA was a long journey. Fifteen years ago, when I lived in my country Afghanistan, I did not even think of coming to the USA. My family and I lived in a house that we rented. As people know, my country was involved in a civil war. We decided to leave our native country and immigrate to our neighboring country, Pakistan. We had not planned to make our lives in another country, but war forced us to leave our country, the country we were born in, grew up in, and went to school in. No one wants to leave his home and live in his neighbor's house, but we had to, like so many other people.

Life in Pakistan was difficult. There were no jobs. We had no money, so my father and my thirteen-year-old brother worked in construction. They earned money to pay the rent and the electricity bill, and to buy food and clothes. We lived with little money, but we were happy because there was not any gunfire. After a while, little by little, we felt safe and started to attend English language courses. My brother and my little sister started to go to school. My father got a job in a factory, and my brother worked in a restaurant.

After a year in Pakistan, I received a marriage proposal. My husband is related to my aunt's husband who came to our house and talked to my parents about my marrying his second cousin. Due to our living situation, my parents decided to have me get engaged to him even though he lived far away. My parents knew my life would be better in the United States. After an engagement period, I got married. The month after my wedding, I came to the USA. I was happy and sad at the same time: happy because I was going to live with my husband in a country of opportunity and sad because my family would be far away. I was going thousands of miles away from them. When I thought about leaving them, I would ask myself a question: Am I going to see them again?

I left the family that I was raised with and all my relatives. I would have to start everything fresh. When I first got to the USA, I was sad and thought about my family and my relatives. It was difficult for me at first, but my husband was with me. He made me feel special. He made me laugh, and he took me places for vacation. He helped me learn how to drive. That was another freedom. Before long, I had my first child. It was a very special, memorable moment of my life. The first time I held her was a beautiful moment, something that I can't quite explain.

As I got busy with my daughter, I did not miss my family as much because I had started my own family in the United States. I still think of my family every day, and I pray to God that some day we can all get together and live in the same country again like we used to.

## Our Place

RAN LU

THE UNITED STATES IS THE dream country in the minds and souls of most people in the world. Living in the USA was the same for me, a beautiful longing, a hope in the heart of a little girl. Now our family has moved here to the United States to make our dreams come true.

Meeting the United States is a story that began with the meeting of my husband and me. My husband, Jinsong, had worked in California since 2001 when he graduated with his MBA from the University of Illinois and moved west. Thousands of miles away from California, I was working in Beijing, China. From across the Pacific Ocean, how did we meet each other?

It was a summer holiday in 2006. He left his hometown to fly to Beijing to catch an international flight back to the USA, and I was on the same flight going from my hometown back to Beijing. It was raining when the plane landed at the Beijing airport. Making my way off the plane, I stood for a moment under the protection of the plane door, just in front of him, to take out my umbrella. He, however, did not take out an umbrella, and naturally, I shared my umbrella with him. That's the beginning of our romantic story.

In late 2006, we were married in Beijing. Because of my job, we spent two years living apart. Finally after much struggle, we decided to make our home in the United States. On May 18, 2008, I moved away from China, from all my relatives and friends, from everything familiar. Before that day in May, I had only visited the United States once for a three-week vacation.

Last year I was pregnant with our first baby. In China, most hospitals are crowded. People can't make an appointment with a doctor by phone, but have to go in person to ask if the doctor has time, and after that, keep waiting and waiting and waiting. In the United States, the experience was different for me. Even before I arrived, Jinsong had chosen a doctor and a clinic online. The Palo Alto Medical Foundation was famous and familiar to him. After I got pregnant, I made an appointment with Dr. Ngo, the obstetrician in the Fremont Center. Every three weeks I went to the center to have some tests. I felt very comfortable in the quiet building with my doctor and midwife, both professional and caring. They told me everything I needed to know. I followed their advice and exercised at least thirty minutes every day, walking outside, swimming, or doing stretches and yoga. I took pregnancy vitamins every day.

During my pregnancy, I was happy and cheerful. After nine months, the most important time came. As you know, delivering a baby is the challenge of a woman's lifetime. I thought it was fortunate for my little baby and me that we were in America. The medical conditions and techniques were modern and powerful. My husband was beside me, and there were plenty of medical professionals on the scene, too. On November 5, 2008, our little William was born. As a new mom, I was busy and tired for the first half year, but it was a very precious time for me and my family.

Now, we live in Livermore, such a beautiful and peaceful city in northern California. In China, most people live in apartments. Our apartment in Beijing was just 800 square feet, but we were really lucky to have that much room. Our house here is not only large, but it is also surrounded by a beautiful yard, something we could never have imagined in China. This spring we planted a peach tree and some vegetables such as onions, tomatoes, and green beans. I like to do some gardening work with my little William in the afternoon. While I am busy watering, planting, and catching snails, he sits in a little chair, looks at me, and sometimes gives me a beautiful smile. I think he is a nature lover, as his father and I are.

Today is a hot summer day, and our peaches are growing pink and fat. Our house is as wonderful as the city around it, blue skies, clear air, friendly people, a quiet public library, a big shopping mall. Everything is wonderful. I love living here.

I have been living in the USA for just one year, but every experience has been unforgettable. My hope is that our family's American dream will grow better and better as the future unfolds.

# Enjoying California

SERGEY KOZLOV

FOR MANY PEOPLE WHO COME to the USA every year for living or business purposes, there are a lot of new discoveries about America, its lifestyle, culture and habits. Some of them are expected and predicted by newcomers, but some of them are not. Sometimes there are even negative impressions. I came to the United States more than two years ago in order to work here. My original expectations of the life here have almost been matched with the realities I've experienced. One of the things which I did not expect to find here is the variety in the natural landscape and the climate zones all over California. My most memorable discovery was made on the coast of the Pacific Ocean and in the mountains of the Sierra Nevada.

The first time I came here and stepped out the doors of the San Francisco International Airport, I realized that the air here was dry and quite hot. I started thinking that this temperature and the humidity level were everywhere else in the golden state. In reality, I was mistaken. I found this out very quickly when a friend of mine took me on a trip to the ocean. It was the first time that I felt the salty air of the Pacific, its fresh breeze, and that tasty smell of ocean greens. It is a strange mix of aromas: ocean water with ocean-side trees and plants. I remember that moment very well. I was standing on the top of cliffs overlooking the ocean, smelling the fresh air with closed eyes and listening to the sounds of the waves. It took me a while to return to reality and realize that my friend was trying to say something to me. Apparently, I hadn't been answering his attempts at communication. It was an unforgettable moment for me, and I still keep a taste of that air in my memory.

The second time I experienced the diversity in California's geography and climate was in the mountains. It happened when friends invited my wife and me for a weekend trip to their mountain cabin near Lake Tahoe. We were planning to stay there for a couple of nights and spend some time at a local ski resort. The cabin was located in a secluded place, far away from towns, in the middle of nowhere, in the mountains. It was built between two big forested hills on the side of a small creek with fresh, cold water. On the morning after our arrival in the mountains, I woke up early and decided to take a short walk around. It was very early; everybody else was still sleeping. I had hoped that my promenade would be quiet and enjoyable, but I had not expected that it would be so wonderful. I was walking in complete silence and tranquility. The only sound which I was able to hear was the sound of flowing water in the creek. That sound was so unusual and pleasant for me that I suddenly stopped walking and tried to hear every note of its song. It was like a small musical instrument was playing some melody under my feet. For some moments, I thought that it would be a great idea to record these sounds and give them to my wife and my friends to listen to when they woke up later that morning. As I was standing there oblivious to time passing, trying to catch the sounds of the creek and the aromas of the forest, I didn't notice at first that I was getting cold. I decided to finish my walk and let everybody know how beautiful the weather outside was. This was the second unforgettable time when I was impressed by the nature and weather of California.

Many people expect different things from their new home or their temporary working place. Some of them expect more than the reality, others less. But I'm sure that everybody who comes to California will enjoy its nature and weather from the bays of the Pacific Ocean to the forests and creeks of the Sierra Nevada. You won't find any place in the world with such impressive variation as you can see and experience in California.

## California Passion

DMITRY IGNATYUK

MY FIRST VISIT TO THE USA happened in the late nineties, a long time ago now. I came to visit my friend and celebrate the New Year here in California. Despite the fact I had experienced some other countries with wonderful places already, I fell in love with this place, California, almost immediately. It's hard to explain, like any other love, but this fantastic combination is breathtaking: the industrial style in the center of San Francisco; the relaxed atmosphere of surrounding cities like Walnut Creek, where the scent of coffee and steak pour into the evening air; the marvelous landscapes of vineyards in the Napa Valley; the people, activities, opportunities, and technology born here. All this and more makes California pretty much the most unique place in the whole world.

You can find almost everything you can imagine here in California and still spend many years discovering new sides of this beautiful area you hadn't imagined. Every single place on the planet has its unique style, which can be described in a couple of phrases and are often tightly associated in everybody's mind with certain geography. What place would you think of if you heard "city of love," "the ancient pyramids," or "the ruined coliseum?" Certainly, every city or country in the world has something that local citizens are proud of, something that attracts tourists, and something that looks nice on the local postcards.

But how can we describe San Francisco or California in a couple of phrases? Can we call it "the city of the Golden Gate Bridge?" Definitely, yes, but it is much more than this. Do you want to find gorgeous mountains or gigantic ancient trees? It's all here, within a three hour drive from San Francisco. Do you want to go camping and see a beautiful ocean sunset from your tent? You can be at that seaside campground in no time; it is here in California. Do you love the nightlife of a big city? As long as you don't forget to pay the four-dollar toll to cross one of the bridges into San Francisco, you can experience all the excitement and mystery of a night out in the big city. Do you like to try interesting foods from all over the world? Here they are, more than one-hundred-thousand restaurants in the Bay Area, all more than happy to serve you dinner. Do you want to feel like you're in Europe? Here it is, this small city called Solvang with windmills, beer, and sour cabbage.

The local communities are pretty much open for communication here in California, which is not necessarily true for other countries. Local people and their cultural activities usually bring something special to every city and every country. What do you think people look like in India, China, or Germany? What do they do every day? Definitely, you can imagine a picture, and some associations will immediately pop up in your mind.

Now let's address the same questions about California. For me, these questions are much more difficult to answer here because you can find everything and everybody from all over the world. Quite often, immigrants live within a very tight community, speaking the same language and creating a comfortable native environment. It's good for certain people, and it is possible to do this in California, but often not quite achievable in other countries. But for those people who are willing to venture out beyond those comforts and boundaries, they will find California an absolutely precious jewel. You can celebrate a sacred Indian spring ritual and end up with your clothes and face painted with colors like all the Indians around you. You can go on hikes or bike rides with people who were born here and find local culture very interesting. Are you interested in the Chinese New Year celebration? You needn't go to China; it also happens right here in many cities and towns all over California.

It is also worth mentioning the intellectual side of California, where many technologies and opportunities have been born. Indeed, it is hard to find another place where the creation of new, interesting ideas happens so quickly. If you drive along Highway 101 from San Francisco south towards San Jose, you will observe a lot of historical places from your car windows. For example, there is a hangar where space shuttles are assembled alongside NASA's Blue Cube, from which all moon expeditions were controlled. Along this same stretch of highway, you can spot the most famous software and Internet company offices: Intel, Oracle, or Google. If you look more closely, you can see the people coming and going from these offices. Those people are the real hearts of Google and Intel, and you can be one of them. We are all constructing the future here, too. To the north of San Francisco, you will discover a lot of new office buildings among experimental farms. Those lands will eventually become a biotechnology valley in a decade or so. All those opportunities also attract a lot of other businesses and more smart people to California.

When I have an early morning flight, quite often I have breakfast in a San Francisco airport restaurant called Perry's. Here I read, engraved on the restaurant's walls, quotations about California by famous people, and I understand that I'm not alone in my passion about this place. I like this one: "If angels bring me to heaven after I die, I'll look around and say — well, this is good, but it ain't San Francisco." I can't agree more with this person, and I think this is a great place to be, in this gorgeous mix of beautiful nature, different cultures, and right on the cutting-edge of technology's frontier.

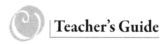 

# Using *One World Many Voices*

Both intensive and extensive reading are important aspects of an ESL reading curriculum. The essays in *One World Many Voices* are designed to provide interesting and easy extensive reading material. They can, however, be used effectively in many ways in the classroom. While extensive reading contributes to overall language proficiency growth and helps students to become successful readers, intensive reading provides instructor-led activities that help students develop reading proficiency and confidence.

Teachers can address factors that lead to unsuccessful and successful reading in the classroom through both intensive and extensive reading activities. Extensive reading alone will not remedy unsuccessful reading practices, but a combination of extensive reading and teacher-led intensive reading activities will remedy most.

## FACTORS IN SUCCESSFUL AND UNSUCCESSFUL READING

### Factors in Unsuccessful Reading

- Lack of rapid, automatic, and accurate word recognition
- Limited sight vocabulary
- Lack of phonological competence
- Limited grasp of the structure of the language
- Inability to disambiguate information in the text
- Inability to use reading strategies flexibly while reading
- Lack of general world knowledge
- Lack of interaction between textual and general world knowledge
- Rigidity in perception and conceptualization

## Factors in Successful Reading

- Rapid, automatic, and accurate word recognition
- Large recognition vocabulary
- Reasonable grasp of the structure of the language
- Ability to disambiguate information
- Ability to establish a standard of coherence, monitor comprehension, set goals, and use strategies to reach that standard
- Ability to integrate meaning
- Ability to make inferences and connections to background knowledge
- Ability to suppress less important information
- Fluency in processing words, sentences, and discourse cues

### EXTENSIVE READING

Extensive reading can help second language readers overcome some factors that lead to unsuccessful reading. Guided extensive reading programs provide readers with carefully selected material and suggestions for reading frequency. They promote reading fluency much the way that journal writing helps students become fluid writers. Most significantly, extensive reading provides reading practice. It guides time-on-task for readers who might not be self-motivated.

### Material

In order to promote fluency, extensive reading material should be easy to read with few unfamiliar words and easy-to-process sentence structure. Students should be able to read faster than they read for intensive reading and should be encouraged not to use a dictionary. The purpose of extensive reading is general understanding.

The essays in these collections are carefully edited for different proficiency levels of English learners. The vocabulary increases in breadth from the most frequent 500 words to the most frequent 2,000 words in English across the series. The sentence structure also increases in complexity over the collection.

The essays in *Living in the USA* were edited for sentence structure and vocabulary to provide high-intermediate level students with interesting and easy to read extensive reading material.

Each book in the series can provide a portion of the required extensive reading material for one semester. At every level of proficiency, students should engage in extensive reading four to five times a week in addition to the reading they do in class.

## The Teacher's Role

Teachers can encourage, inspire, and motivate students to read by engaging in extensive reading along with their students in the classroom and by establishing an expectation of extensive reading outside of the classroom. Teachers are excellent models for reading and discussing books. They can share their own experiences with reading and tell students about the books they are reading. When teachers read the same books that the students are reading, they can share their reactions to the books and guide student discussions. Language learners often have limited experience reading in English or discussing things they read in their new language. The teacher can model these activities and encourage students to discuss their reading with each other.

Teachers might introduce extensive reading with activities that invite students to examine their reading experiences, habits, and attitudes toward reading in their first language.

## Goals of Extensive Reading

Extensive reading can help second language readers overcome some factors that lead to unsuccessful reading practices. The goals of extensive reading include the following:

- Improve reading comprehension
- Increase rapid, automatic, and accurate recognition of the most frequent English words
- Encourage incidental vocabulary learning
- Increase reading rate
- Gain overall language proficiency
- Build general knowledge
- Support the development of a reader identity in English
- Establish a community of readers

# Suggestions for Teacher-Directed Activities

The essays in *Living in the USA* can be used as a classroom resource not only for extensive reading practice, but also for achieving extensive reading goals. They are a resource for practicing reading skills and strategies that promote successful reading. The following suggestions have emerged from our experience using the essays in the classroom. We hope that you find them useful.

### IMPROVE COMPREHENSION

Book discussions can help readers of English develop a sense of competence and autonomy as they read for comprehension. Discussion activities can help them monitor their comprehension and motivate them to develop comprehension strategies. Such strategies include re-reading, looking for key words or ideas, constructing mental summaries, and connecting ideas encountered in the text to their own experiences. Here are some activities that can help learners improve their comprehension.

- After reading a passage once, tell a partner about the passage without looking at the text.
- Read a passage multiple times and tell a partner about the passage without looking at the text. Discuss the comprehension differences after a third or fourth reading.
- Connect the ideas in an essay to personal experience.
- Identify the most important ideas in an essay.
- In pairs or small groups, discuss an essay in light of similarities and/or differences with personal experience.

## LEARN AND PRACTICE READING STRATEGIES

Students learn reading strategies from their reading textbooks and practice applying those strategies during teacher-guided activities in class. The essays in this book can provide additional practice opportunities for mastering those strategies and for supporting their integration into students' independent reading practices. Here are some activities that can provide learners with opportunities to practice various reading strategies.

- Ask students to preview the book and discuss its overall organization as a class.
- After reading a chapter, ask students to work in pairs or small groups to draw inferences about one or more of the essays. For example, students might be asked to draw inferences about cultural expectations or values not explicitly discussed in an essay.
- Ask students to discuss their previous knowledge or experience with a topic from one of the chapters. For example, ask students to tell about their arrival in the USA or how their attitudes have changed since their arrival.
- Ask students to scan for particular information. For example, students might scan a passage for key words or ideas.
- Select one essay in a chapter and ask students to look for transition signals, key words, or other coherence devices that link ideas from within and between paragraphs.

## INCREASE READING RATE

Slow readers spend a great deal of time processing individual letters and words, making it difficult for them to understand what they are reading. Reading faster will aid comprehension and increase reading pleasure. It will also contribute to overall academic success. English language learners will naturally increase their reading speed over time as their general language proficiency increases, but with practice and guidance their reading speed can increase more quickly. Here are some activities that can help students increase their reading speed.

### Reading Pairs

1. Select a passage from the book. Ask students to work with a partner.
2. Partner A reads aloud for 30 seconds.
3. Partner B reads the same passage for 30 seconds.
4. Repeat.
5. Ask how many more words were read each time.

### Reading Sprints

1. Select a passage from the book. Ask students to read silently for four minutes. Use a timer or a watch with a second hand. Then ask them to count the number of lines they read.
2. Students then count out the same number of lines in the next part of the passage. They continue reading for three minutes, trying to read the same number of lines in less time. Students count the lines they read in three minutes, count out the same number of lines in the next part of the passage, and try to read as many lines in two minutes.
3. When the reading sprint is complete, the class can discuss their comprehension of the text.

### Monitor

1. Encourage students to monitor their reading speed.
2. Have students chart their progress.

## RAPID, ACCURATE, AUTOMATIC WORD RECOGNITION

Increased reading comprehension and reading speed are only possible when students can rapidly and accurately recognize large numbers of words in print. Their vocabulary for listening and speaking is not accessed for reading unless they also recognize what a word looks like on the printed page and then connect that word to their mental lexicon. Extensive reading exposes language learners to the printed word, but it does not ensure that students accurately process the correct meaning. Some read aloud activities can help language learners connect printed words to the vocabulary they have developed for listening and speaking. It can also provide consistent pronunciation practice.

### Read Aloud

- After students read a passage silently twice, ask them to read it aloud to a partner.
- Assign one paragraph of a passage to each student. For homework the student should practice reading aloud, focusing on careful pronunciation and phrasing. In class, students read to each other.

### Pronunciation

- Encourage students to use the computer software or Internet interface of an English language learner dictionary and ensure that students know the pronunciation of the a large number of the most frequent English words.
- Encourage students to say and write words to promote the connection between the written and spoken forms.
- Make pronunciation an important part of knowing a word.

## ENCOURAGE INCIDENTAL LEARNING AND DEEPEN WORD KNOWLEDGE

Sometimes students believe that reading will help their vocabulary development only if reading texts contain many new words. Talking to students about the value of reading easy texts for learning vocabulary may help them see the value of extensive reading more clearly.

Extensive reading can also help students deepen their knowledge of known words since knowing a word includes many types of knowledge such as knowing the spelling, pronunciation, and multiple meanings of the word. Simple activities such as reading aloud, listening and repeating, and listening to audio files of passages can all contribute to deepening learners' knowledge of a word. Teachers can also direct students' attention to words in a passage that draw on less frequent uses of those words.

## LINK READING AND WRITING

Regular journal writing about topics from their reading can promote both reading and writing fluency. Ungraded reflective writing about their ideas after reading promotes close reading, encourages readers to explore reactions to the text, gives them a chance to examine features of a text more closely, and encourages readers to link their own experiences to those of the writer. Here are some possible journal prompts.

- What does the author mean by...?
- How are the experiences of the authors different from or similar to your experiences?
- What did you think about as you read...?
- What was interesting/confusing about this essay/chapter?
- Write about how living in a different culture causes you to change.

INCREASE OVERALL LANGUAGE PROFICIENCY

Listening, speaking, reading, and writing in English all require knowledge of grammar. Reading easy and interesting material, as students do with extensive reading, helps them confirm their knowledge of English grammar and provides extensive input upon which to make further generalizations about English grammar. Here are some activity types that can help learners gain overall language proficiency.

## Sound-Spelling Relationship

- A student whose native language uses a writing system that is very different from the English alphabet will likely benefit from activities that focus attention on sound-spelling relationships.
- Copying a paragraph can give students easy practice with forming letters and spelling.

## Grammar Analysis

Analyzing the grammar in a passage helps students to focus on language structure and to discuss their observations. Each activity should take no more than 15 minutes. The possibilities are endless, but here are some ideas.

1. First, select a paragraph that has a sufficient number of the target structure and make an overhead transparency of the paragraph.
2. Students should first work alone for three minutes to identify as many examples of the target structure as they can.
3. Next, ask students to work in pairs to confirm their findings.
4. Finally show your own findings on the overhead. At the high-intermediate level, students benefit from identifying each clause in the sentences of an essay. They can identify the subject and verb in each clause. They could also identify the verb tense in each clause and speculate on the other verb tenses that might also work. They can identify noun phrases, prepositional phrases, subject phrases, and verb phrases. They can find pronouns and referents, gerunds and infinitives, and participle phrases. They can analyze the punctuation, and they can also make generalizations about articles by observing them in the text.

## DEVELOP FLUENCY

Reading fluency and speaking fluency often develop at different rates. When students have opportunities to talk about what they are reading, they bring together multiple skills. The activities below also encourage integrating reading and speaking skills as well as multiple readings of a text, which can deepen understanding and enable readers to see something new with each reading.

### Read Aloud

Students should read a passage silently multiple times and rehearse before reading it aloud to a partner.

### Oral Summaries

Students retell passages from memory and confirm comprehension.

1. Students read one entry as many times as they can for 10–12 minutes.
2. With a partner, retell/summarize the passage.
3. Identify key points with the whole class.
4. Read the passage again.

### Summary Sprints

In pairs, students summarize a passage.

1. Student A has three minutes to summarize the passage.
2. Student B has two minutes to summarize the same passage.
3. Student A has one minute to summarize the same passage.

 | **Teacher's Guide**

BUILD GENERAL KNOWLEDGE

Each chapter in *Living in the USA* includes both personal experience and information about the writer's culture. This diversity of experiences provides geographical, cultural, religious, and family perspectives and provides an opportunity for readers to develop knowledge about cultures and countries very different from their own. They can confirm their new knowledge through discussion activities or research assignments.

ENGAGE IN CRITICAL THINKING

Students need practice thinking and analyzing as they read. Some simple activities that encourage students to think about organization of ideas and how ideas relate across several essays can help students to do this on their own. Here are some examples of how to use the book to encourage critical thinking.

- Each chapter in the book focuses on an aspect of living in the USA. Select several passages about the same type of experience, and ask students to work in small groups to identify similarities and differences.
- Encourage students to draw conclusions from reading about a particular type of experience. Ask critical thinking questions such as why a particular experience was important to the author, what aspects of the experience reveal something about the author's culture, or what the author does not express that might be important.
- Ask students to select their favorite essay from a given chapter and to tell a group of students the reasons for their opinions.

## SUPPORT READER IDENTITY IN ENGLISH

Developing an identity as an English reader over the course of several semesters can help language learners transition from learning to read to reading to learn. Extensive reading provides the time-on-task that builds confidence, promotes learning, and provides practice. All of these can lead to increased pleasure reading, other types of independent reading, and related oral or written activities that readers engage in as part of what it means to be a reader. Activities that invite students to discuss or write about their experiences as English readers can help them be more aware of their development of an English reader identity.

## CREATE A COMMUNITY OF READERS

Many of us have had the pleasurable experience of talking to friends and colleagues about a book we have read. When we discuss our own reading with others, we become part of a larger community of readers. When language learners engage in reading the same book as part of their extensive reading, they have the opportunity to experience that same pleasure. They share their ideas and participate in a community that values reading and sharing ideas about that reading.

# Countries

AFGHANISTAN
BOLIVIA
BRAZIL
BULGARIA
CAMBODIA
CHECK REPUBLIC
CHINA
COLOMBIA
ECUADOR
GERMANY
HONDURAS
INDONESIA
IRAN
JAPAN
KOREA
MEXICO
PAKISTAN
PERU
PHILIPPINES
RUSSIA
SERBIA
TAIWAN
THAILAND
UKRAINE
VIETNAM

# Index of Authors

*M*ARILYN MARQUIS TEACHES ESL AT Las Positas College in Livermore, California. She was inspired to become an ESL teacher after hosting two young people through the Experiment in International Living. She began teaching English as a Second Language at Long Beach City College in 1983 and was an adjunct English and ESL teacher there until 1991 when she joined the faculty at Las Positas College. Reading instruction has been an area of particular interest to her throughout her professional life. She has enjoyed the collaboration on this series of student-generated essays. Marilyn holds a bachelor's degree in English from California State University, Northridge and a master's degree from California State University, Dominguez Hills.

*S*ARAH NIELSEN HAS BEEN INTERESTED in language learning and teaching since she was a high school student. She spent a year in Belgium living with a French speaking family and attending school before she began her university education. She taught English in China for two years before entering graduate school. She began teaching as an adjunct ESL instructor in 1995 before joining the faculty at Las Positas College in 2000. In 2004, she joined the faculty at California State University, East Bay, as the coordinator of the MA TESOL program. Sarah holds a bachelor's degree from the University of California, Santa Cruz, and both a master's degree, and a Ph.D. from the University of California, Davis.